BOSTON

The small town with a big story

To my wife Alison

*whose knowledge and support has
significantly enhanced this book.*

Richard Austin

First Published 2019

Published by Richard Austin Cherry Tree Books

© Richard Austin, 2019

ISBN 978-1-9161959-0-5

Printing, typesetting and origination by Vinspirational Ltd

Cover photograph by Jaimaneul Freire

FOREWORD

Imagine the scene; there you are in the hustle and bustle of a busy London Underground platform and you are greeted by a poster of Hollywood star Rob Lowe in a police uniform in the middle of a cabbage field next to a sign which says Boston, Lincolnshire.
Underneath scrawled graffiti-like in brackets is the slogan "Not that Boston".

That's the sight which commuters came across as ITV used the notion that Boston America is better known than Boston Lincolnshire to advertise its show Wild Bill, set and filmed in our Boston, as Lowe's character arrives in town to head the local police force.

Thanks to that prime-time comedy drama series, millions of people across the country now know that there is another Boston and it's the original one.

But how many Boston folk actually know about their town and the history on their doorstep?

Well this book attempts to provide some of the answers. Have you ever walked past a building in town and pondered its history? You know the statue outside the Stump is Herbert Ingram but you don't really know much about him. You've been to see a performance at Blackfriars but know little of the story of the building. You've heard of that Matthew Flinders guy but would struggle to explain what he did. Let Boston - The Small Town with a Big Story be your guide.

Endorsed by the Boston Heritage Forum, the book is the result of a year-long labour of love by Richard Austin which has individual writers come together in a team effort to each give their individual take on different aspects of almost 1,000 years of history.

It might even provide some "well I've lived in Boston all my life and I never knew that" moments and could even help settle a pub argument or two about an element of the town's rich heritage.

If only Rob Lowe's character had been given a copy on arrival in Boston he would have been better prepared for his "fish out of water" Wild Bill adventures in the town!

Scott Dalton,
Bostonian and BBC Radio Lincolnshire Breakfast Show presenter.

Boston Stump and the former foot bridge over the Witham

ABOUT THIS BOOK

Boston, Lincolnshire, has a remarkable and rich heritage that has been well documented, although many people would struggle to pinpoint its location. Some better informed people may say it is a city in America that had a famous 'tea party'. Of course, Boston's isolated position on England's east coast has not helped. Because of this, the lack of knowledge has resulted in much of Boston's real story being misrepresented or misunderstood.

Beginning on a muddy creek meandering through fenland marshes on its way to the Wash – that large bay on England's east coast - where salt and whatever else the marshes could provide to sustain a meagre existence, Boston emerged in time as an important trading centre. Its relative isolation made its people self-sufficient, independently minded and often adventurous.

Over the intervening centuries, its people helped lay the foundations of the United States of America, map newly discovered lands on the other side of the world, tame the local fenlands and revolutionise farming and food production in the UK. They even took the lead in producing the humble 'duvet', essential for that good night's sleep.

The book takes the reader on a journey through time, in a series of stories that combine to present an overall picture of the town and the impact its people have made - and are making - upon the world of today. Carefully selected photographs, illustrations and maps supplement the text. It has been a huge team effort – a team of editors, writers and other contributors who want to share with others what is special about Boston.

The story of Boston is a never ending story of people, of their triumphs and disasters, of their innovations, dreams and the striving for a better future. But we hope this book will give you, the reader, a starting point for your own journey through Boston - the small town with a big story.

Richard Austin
David Radford

Boston Town Bridge c 1790 drawn by CW Pilcher

ACKNOWLEDGEMENTS

The production of this book has been a team effort, and the editors would like to thank all those who have contributed toward creating a book all can be proud of.

Particular thanks go to the Boston Heritage Forum for endorsing the project; to our writers: Adam Cartwright, Alison Fairman, Andrew Hoyle, Andrew Malkin, Ann Carlton, Chris Andrews, David Haycock, Ian Middleton, James Waterfall, Jill Pepper, John Debnam, John Gray, Judy Cammack, Dr Ken Hines, Luke Skerritt, Dr Martyn Walling, Patrick Corke, Robert Barclay, Robert Fleet, Roy Hackford, Shane Bagley, Sharon Middleton, Shirley Rogers, Suesan Brown and Tom Lane; to our American colleagues Barry Cotton and Eve LaPlante and to local historian Neil Wright, both for his written contribution and advice. Thanks also go to Steve Johnston for his excellent maps, artists Mary Findell, Jane Robson and Kerry Ellis, and Betty Brammer, Brenda Lane and Frank and Sally Dowser for their research.

We have been fortunate to receive the support of many image archives. These have included the British Library Board, the British Museum, The Lancaster City Museum, The National Museum of Lithuania, The Salvation Army International Heritage Centre and British Swimming. The work of our photographers and the willingness of those with local photo collections to assist us has been unstinting: Alison Fairman, Andy Lamming, Bryan S Graves, Chris Sidebottom, Ian Moore, Jaimanuel Freire, Jim Blaylock, Keith Ian Smith, Martijn Cornelissen, Mike Peberdy, Neil Smith, Neil Watson, Pamela Cawthorne, Robert Munslow, Ron Jessop and Roy Hackford. Thanks also goes to Richard Starbuck for enhancing the quality of many of the book's images.

Our final thanks go to those who have provided support in a variety of ways, each essential to the completion of the overall project. These include Peter Atlee, The Black Sluice and Witham Fourth Drainage Boards, St Botolph's Church, The Guildhall Museum and Polly Wilkinson, Adrian Isaac and Boston Woods Trust, Boston Borough Council, the Joseph Banks Centre, Blackfriars Theatre, Boston in Bloom, the Boston Preservation Trust, Fydell House, the Inshore Fisheries and Conservation Association, Johnsons Seeds, the RSPB, the We'll Meet Again Museum, Freiston, The Lincolnshire & Nottinghamshire Air Ambulance, Calders and Grandidge Ltd, Metsä and the Boston Hanse Group.

We are grateful to Vinny and Holly of Vinspirational Ltd, the designers of this book, for their work in bringing to life everyone's hard work; to proof readers John Radford and Julian Kirby, and last, but by no means least, the support of our wives Alison and Ann who have been tireless advisors, script checkers and a source of encouragement throughout the process. If we have omitted anyone deserving our thanks we are truly sorry. Any mistakes are our own.

Richard Austin
David Radford

CONTENTS

SALT EXTRACTION
Tom Lane

Salt has always been a valuable commodity and long before there was ever a town called Boston the people who inhabited its fenlands were engaged in extracting salt from the sea. There is evidence of salt-making going back to the Iron Age and its production didn't stop until the early seventeenth century, more than 1,600 years later. The most obvious remains are the mounds of discarded silt in such places as Bicker and Quadring that now grow crops and mark where the old salt workings were during the medieval period. It was a vast enterprise. Monasteries played a big part in Lincolnshire salt making.

Many acres of rolling fields created by the discard from this industry can also be seen around Wrangle. The light coloured areas on the LiDAR map show the extent of these hills, known as tofts, in an otherwise flat landscape. At one time they would have been even higher, but intensive agriculture has reduced their height over the years.

A site where salt was made was called a saltern and the process comprised three main parts.

- The first was to collect salt-rich mud from the shores and estuaries after the spring tides
- This salty mud was placed on top of a bed of turves and peat. Water was poured in and a pipe took the filtrate to a clay-lined collecting tank
- Finally, salt was produced by evaporating this brine in lead pans over peat fires.

Salt Extraction Spoil Heaps
The yellow areas of these LiDAR images show the site of spoil heaps left by the salt workers. It is now fertile arable land standing above the surrounding landscape.

Where possible water was used to aid the filtration process through turves or peat as this dissolved the desired sodium chloride. Some unwanted salts such as Epsom Salts remained. The desalinated silty mud was then taken away and discarded in spoil heaps. The huge volume of waste silts indicates the industry's large scale. Even today dark areas of soil caused by ash from the boiling process can still be seen in the fields in the Borough.

In the Iron Age and Roman periods and into the eighth-century, salt was made in a much simpler way, as is evidenced by Saxon archaeology at Fishtoft.

- Firstly peat was dug, dried and transported on to the site for fuel

- Clay was then excavated and made into pans or troughs

- Brine was collected from entrapment ditches and transferred to settling tanks to allow sediment to fall out

- The final process was evaporation in a line of clay troughs placed over hearths burning peat

- The resultant salt was moved either in carts, or by boats.

Until about the mid-fourteenth century there was a considerable export trade in salt from Boston and other Lincolnshire ports, after which cheaper salt began to be imported.

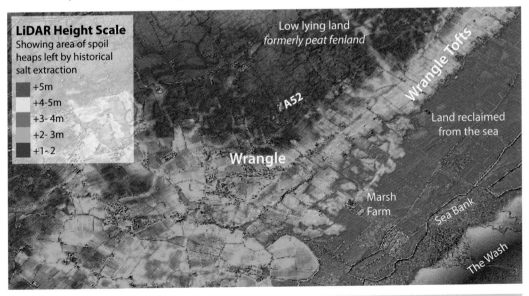

LiDAR Height Scale
Showing area of spoil heaps left by historical salt extraction

- +5m
- +4-5m
- +3- 4m
- +2-3m
- +1- 2

Low lying land
formerly peat fenland

Wrangle Tofts

A52

Land reclaimed from the sea

Wrangle

Marsh Farm

Sea Bank

The Wash

More Information: *Minerals from the Marshes by Tom Lane.*

THE NORMAN TAKEOVER
David Radford

Boston began as part of Skirbeck, unlike today when it is the other way round. The Normans turned it into a thriving settlement they called 'St Botolph's Town' after a saint who had been given land by the River Witham for a monastery. It was shortened around the year 1400 to 'Boston'.

The medieval stone carving of St Botolph keeps watch over the town from the 'Stump' (drawing by CW Pilcher).

In 1066 three people claimed the throne of England after the death of Edward the Confessor. Harold II who was chosen by the English earls and crowned their new king; Harald Hardrada, king of Norway; and William of Normandy who claimed that Edward the Confessor had promised him the throne. At this time Boston was an insignificant settlement in the Skirbeck Hundred where ancient fenland routes crossed the River Witham. The Lord of the Manor was Ralph, a leading Saxon nobleman known as the Constable. Its inhabitants had a strong Viking heritage and more than half were sokemen, peasants with considerable personal freedoms.

While William was making preparations to invade England, Hardrada landed in the Humber estuary. Earl Edwin, King Harold's brother-in law, led the men of Lincolnshire against him but they were beaten. However Harold soon arrived and defeated the invaders at the Battle of Stamford Bridge. By this time, however, William had landed in England and Harold rushed south. In the ensuing battle at Hastings the Saxon army was destroyed and Harold was killed.

In the years that followed the Normans took control of the country building castles and ruthlessly supressing any resistance, including Hereward the Wake and his fenland guerrillas. William divided up England between himself and his supporters. He gave them new titles and made them swear an oath of loyalty to him, known as the Oath of Salisbury. So none became too powerful William scattered their new lands throughout England. He made a list called the Domesday Book so he knew exactly what tax they should pay and what military service they should give him.

Boston and the surrounded area was split many ways. The Count of Brittany, nicknamed Alan the Red, because of his red beard, became the Earl Richmond. His lands included Ralph's manor at Skirbeck that

Crowland Abbey

Count Alan Rufus receiving the Honour of Richmond from William the Conqueror © The British Library Board (A80109-59 Cotton Faustina B. VII .f.72v)

covered all Boston's east bank. The 'Skirbeck Quarter' went to Eudo, son of Sperwic, and Guy de Croun received the land on the west side of the river. The Croun family later married into the de Roos family; Rosegarth Street, Boston, and Roos Hall, Frieston are named after them. Villages such as Wyberton, Frampton and Fishtoft were split between the de Croun's and the Earl of Richmond. Bicker was shared between the Earl, Guy de Croun, the Archbishop of York and Countess Judith.

Countess Judith, niece of William the Conqueror, married the Saxon Earl Waltheof in 1070. He had been a supporter King Harold but changed sides after the Battle of Hastings. In 1075 he became involved in a rebellion against William and when Judith found out she told William. Waltheof was arrested and executed. He was secretly buried in Crowland Abbey by its monks who later included his effigy when the abbey was rebuilt. Countess Judith inherited the Earl's lands that included a manor at Bicker where she lived for a time.

The Norman Conquest set Boston on course to become the tenth richest town in England. Yet, in spite of the changes, one thing remained constant: the independence inherited from its Viking past. This would one day inspire the creation of a new and grander Boston on the other side of the Atlantic.

More Information: Boston, 1086-1225, A Medieval town by Stephen H. Rigby; The Domesday Book Online; The Story of Boston by Richard Gurnham

MARKETS AND FAIRS
Sharon Middleton

Medieval Boston was a prosperous town with a busy port. It was very wealthy. Only London paid more in tax than Boston. While much of this wealth was generated by the port, the town was also important for its markets and fairs. Regular markets enabled people from the surrounding area to buy and sell goods and services, whilst its fairs, dating from about 1125, had an international reputation. A royal charter of 1218 recorded the town's right to hold markets and fairs, with further charters being issued to confirm Boston's rights and privileges as a trading centre.

Boston's annual fairs were sumptuous occasions. Lasting several days, velvet and silk, wines and spice, fish and all manner of luxury goods from Europe and further afield were traded. Whilst these fairs were important, the weekly markets were equally so. The Saturday Market was established by a charter of 1308. In 1545 when the Corporation of Boston was established, the town was granted the right to hold twice weekly markets, adding a Wednesday livestock market. Wednesdays and Saturdays are still the town's market days.

Cattle Market (Neil Watson Collection)

Although the trade coming through the port declined from about 1500, the town remained a prosperous trading hub. During the 1570s the weekly market was so busy that stallholders had to be segregated according to their merchandise, and armed guards employed to keep the peace.

The sheep fair in Wide Bargate c 1800

Following the drainage of thousands of acres around Boston, the importance of livestock increased and the annual sheep fair held in Wide Bargate during May became an important fixture in the calendar. In the 1820s the town's fair was held in August, a horse and cattle fair took place in November and a cattle fair occurred in December. This remained the pattern until the agricultural slump of the late 1880s from which the livestock fairs never recovered.

In 1732 an elegant new Butter Cross was erected to serve as a market exchange with assembly rooms above. A very smart Corn Exchange was built in 1855, but it was never used as such because farmers and merchants preferred to carry out their business in huts in the market place, as they had always done.

As the prosperity of the eighteenth century progressed, many Bostonians were setting up shops in the town. In 1784 there were 35 shopkeepers but by 1835 there were 910! Despite this increase in the number of shops, the weekly market continued to flourish. The fairs were also good for business, particularly for the taverns, of which Boston had many. By the 1890s the May Fair's growing emphasis on entertainment saw showmen setting up the latest rides and amusements alongside the market stalls, a tradition that is still strong today.

A typical town market stall (Bryan S. Graves)

All the fun of the fair (Bryan S. Graves)

More Information: Boston: Its Story & people by George S Bagley; The Story of Boston by Richard Gurnham

BOSTON AND THE HANSEATIC LEAGUE
Alison Fairman

Hanse Merchant

The Hanseatic League was a powerful trading alliance of merchant guilds or trade associations led by the German merchants of Lubeck that dominated trade along the northern coasts of Europe from the 12th to the 17th-century. Their boats, known as 'cogs' were well built from Baltic oak and were designed to carry a large cargo. The biggest could be 25 metres long and 8 metres wide. In many towns they used, the League established a *kontor*, a trading centre with offices and warehouses built around a courtyard. In England these were known as steelyards from the German *stålhof*, a place where goods were offered for sale.

Boston was an ideal port from which the Hanseatic League could conduct its business. It was on the East coast facing Europe and the Baltic with river access to much of England. Boston soon became an important part of the Hanse network that included places such as London, Lynn and Hull. Boston's famous international fair was frequented by merchants from all over Europe.

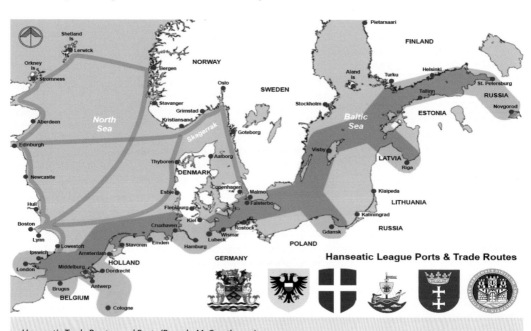

Hanseatic Trade Routes and Ports (Pamela M. Cawthorne)

Replica of a Hanse trading ship or Cog (Mike Peberdy)

Wool was the dominant export. Fountains Abbey was the largest and richest wool producer in northern England and its monks owned property in Fountains Lane in Boston. There were also links to many other monasteries such as Kirkstead and Louth and even as far away as Furness in Cumbria. The Wool Staple was the place through which all wool exports had to pass. When it was transferred from Lincoln to Boston in 1369 trade increased and by 1377 Boston was second only to London as the busiest port in the country. Between 1379-1388 Boston exported 37% of English wool, about three million fleeces per year.

The Hanseatic Steelyard in Boston was located at South End near the Dock. The Mart Yard, now the Grammar School yard, was near the river quayside and this part of town was the original site for markets. The 'Esterlings', as these foreign traders from Germany were sometimes known, had strong links with the Franciscans whose Friary was nearby. One merchant, Wisselus de Smalenburg, was buried in their cemetery in 1312 and his body later interred inside St Botolph's.

By the 1380s the cloth trade in Boston was dominated by Hanseatic merchants who also traded in wines, wax, dried fish, furs, goat skins and hawks. However, trading began to decline as merchants left the town. By the end of the 15th-century there was open hostility between the Hanseatic League and the English crown leading to the cessation of all Hanse trade. The unrest created in Boston led to one of the Esterlings being killed by Humphrey Littleburye. Although the Treaty of Utrecht in 1474 restored some trade, the Hanse merchants seldom visited the port again, and by 1481, the Hanse house was dilapidated and the Steelyard abandoned.

Children experiencing archaeology first hand during the Big Dig 2019 on the site of Boston's Hanse Steelyard (Ian Moore)

Although the Hanseatic League was dissolved in 1669, a 'New Hansa' was formed at Zwolle, The Netherlands in 1984. Boston joined in 2015, making visits to several other 'Hanse Tag', promoting the town and giving opportunity for the youth members to meet other young people.

More Information: *Rediscovering England's Hanseatic Heritage: Medieval Boston, by Pamela M. Cawthorne*

ST BOTOLPH'S CHURCH
Judy Cammack

Rising skywards from the flat landscape of the Fens, St Botolph's Church is a monument to the town's past and a landmark for its future. Known by most as the Stump, it is arguably the largest parish church in England. Dedicated to St Botolph, an Anglo-Saxon Benedictine monk who in the 7th- century is believed to have founded the original church.

St Botolph's Church, known locally as 'the Stump'
(Jaimaneul Freire)

The present church reflects the prosperity of medieval Boston with its foundation stone having been laid in 1309 by Margaret (or Maude) Tilney, wife of one of the leading citizens. Built on some thirty feet of silt, the building had to be stabilised in the 15th century by adding two bays to the chancel. The tower, whose foundations are on solid boulder clay left by the last ice age and five feet deeper than the bed of the river was completed around 1520. An amazing feat of engineering that is still less than 1cm out of vertical.

Until Henry VIII's reformation up to 33 priests from the religious houses and guilds were believed to have been attached to the church. Holding 1500 people (no seats back then), it would have been colourful, with brasses, gilded ceilings and coloured woodwork. During the reign of Edward VI all the decorations were obliterated, the Guild chapel destroyed and the bells removed. In 1538 the great rood cross was taken down and burned in the Market Place.

The pulpit seen today was installed in 1612. It is known as Cotton's Pulpit after the Rev John Cotton, the puritan whose services had long sermons and no music. In 1634, not long after Cotton's departure for Boston, Massachusetts, the new Archbishop of Canterbury, William Laud, founded the Library. With the coming of the English Civil War and the arrival of Oliver Cromwell's cavalry, the church suffered much abuse. Horses were tethered in the north aisle and muskets fired at the walls. Some of the holes resulting are still visible near the Cotton Chapel.

In 1717 a new organ and high box pews were installed, whilst in 1845 a period of restoration, directed by George Gilbert Scott began. The east window was redesigned by George Place, new pews were installed and canopies added to the choir stalls. The stone vaulted ceiling above the great west window in the tower was created and a new Gothic-style font by Augustus Pugin was built. Gifts from Americans funded a redesigned chapel in the south-west corner, which was named in honour of John Cotton.

The Choir and High Altar

Another period of restoration, funded again by American gifts, occurred between 1929 and 1933. Then the tower was straightened, the bells re-cast and the nave re-roofed in a style close to the original 15th century design. Preservation work and modernisation never really ends and in recent days conservation work has included the tower, the west door, the Cotton Chapel and the chancel. New visitor facilities were opened by HRH The Princess Royal in 2012.

The John Cotton Chapel, restored in 1857 by George Gilbert Scott (Bryan S. Graves)

The Font (Bryan S. Graves)

THE 1390 CRUSADE
Andrew Hoyle

In 1390 an armed expedition sailed out of Boston in two ships under the leadership of Henry Bolingbroke, Earl of Derby. The destination was Danzig, where they were to join in a Holy War in defence of Christian lands in northern Europe led by the Teutonic Knights. The Knights were an Order of warrior-monks based in Prussia and the hanseatic centres of Danzig and Konigsberg. Before that, Henry was at the great Inglevert jousting tournament in France and was inspired by the talk amongst the competing knights to join the brotherhood of knights heading for the crusade in Tunisia. But when he was denied safe conduct across France, he readily agreed to join another crusade about to start in Lithuania.

Henry was born in Bolingbroke Castle just north of Boston and was son of the famous John of Gaunt. He was one of the greatest princes in Europe and later to become King Henry IV. His home in the town was Gysors Hall, opposite today's Fydell House.

The expedition left the Haven on 20th July 1390, the feast day of St Margaret. On board the two ships were 16 knights, among whom was Sir Ralph Rochford, of Rochford Tower in Boston. He was one of Gaunt's knights and was paid 8d a day to be part of Henry's retinue. Geoffrey Chaucer, a close friend of John of Gaunt, by reason that they were married to sisters, was a confidant of Henry and probably based the Knight in his Canterbury Tales on Sir Ralph.

Henry Bolingbroke, Earl of Derby, was crowned Henry IV in 1399

"Above the knights of all nations in Prussia
He campaigned in Lithuania and Prussia"
from the prologue, Canterbury Tales, by Geoffrey Chaucer

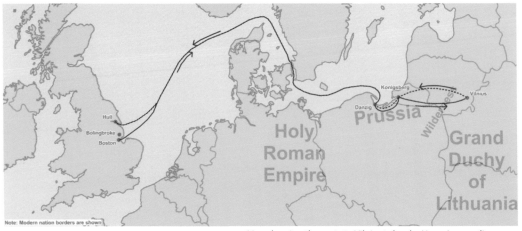

Map showing the route to Vilnius taken by Henry's crusading army

After spending some time in Danzig (Gdansk), the English force of about 300 accompanied by 13 carts carrying their stores and armour left to capture Vilnius, in the Duchy of Lithuania. On the way, in their first battle, they captured three Lithuanian Dukes, 11 high ranking nobles and 200 horses.

Misericord caving in St Botolph's showing the likeness of Henry IV and double headed eagle

When they reached Vilnius they found it heavily defended with outer wooden defences and an inner hill-top stone castle. The city was stormed on 4th September, 1390. Records written at the time say that Henry's English bowmen played a crucial part in the battle and that it was an English yeoman retainer of the Lord Bouchier who planted a banner on the wall of the city. Vilnius was looted and burned and many prisoners taken but the hill-top castle was not captured.

Henry returned to Bolingbroke Castle in October via Hull, sending his baggage back to Boston by boat. In 1392, Henry returned to the Baltic region with a second army, this time sailing from Kings Lynn. He subsequently went on pilgrimage to Jerusalem.

Rochford Manor was formerly Sir Ralph Rochford's home. It was remodelled around 1460 (Pishey Thompson, 1856)

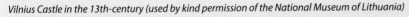

Vilnius Castle in the 13th-century (used by kind permission of the National Museum of Lithuania)

More Information: *Boston's Forgotten Crusade by Andrew Hoyle*

THE FRIARIES
David Radford

For most people in Medieval England, heaven and hell were realities. How to achieve one and avoid the other was of great importance. For those in rural settings where the parish priest exercised strong influence, it was uncomplicated. But in areas of rapid urbanization, where new ideas on religion found fertile ground, the Church was losing control. Among those who saw this clearly was Robert Grosseteste, Bishop of Lincoln. He decided to take some friars with him on his tours of his diocese to address this problem. Boston, with its rapidly growing population and commercial interests was a prime target for his revival. Called the Mendicant Orders, the friars chose to live among ordinary people rather than in monasteries. They were the religious teachers and the medical and social care workers of their day.

Blackfriars, Spain Lane, Boston (F L Griggs, 1914)

The first to settle in Boston were the Dominicans (Order of the Preachers) or Black Friars. Located near the town quay, their Friary included an open-air preaching yard where they gave regular talks. Like the other Orders they were only accountable to the Pope which frequently led to clashes with the parish clergy, bishops and others over their rights. What remains of their buildings is now the Blackfriars Arts Centre.

Boston's Grey Friars (Franciscans) were from the part of that Order dedicated to working in towns. Less confrontational, they settled among the 'Esterlings' (European traders) and took care of the sick and poor of the town. They also put on 'Mystery Plays' which were must see events. Boston Grammar School now occupies their site. This school was founded (endowed) by Queen Mary and Philip of Spain in 1555 and was one of the earliest grammar schools in England. It later became the model for the Latin School, Boston MA, the first school in America.

The Carmelite Order (White Friars) began on Mount Carmel but were driven out of the Holy Land when the Crusaders were defeated. They became refugees and eventually reached England where former crusading families such as Boston's De Roos family helped them. The Order was given an oratory chapel in St Botolph's and eventually built a Friary near Fydell Crescent.

Illustration: Kerry Ellis

The Augustinian Friars (Austins) wanted to help those facing the commercial stresses and crowded living conditions of urban life by teaching about a more contemplative lifestyle. They set up their house on land in Skirbeck which later became the site of Boston's workhouse.

Although based in Whaplode, the 'Crutched Friars' (so called because of the distinctive staff surmounted with a crucifix they carried) would have been a familiar sight in the town. They collected money to pay the ransoms of those seized by pirates and brigands while on pilgrimage.

While the Friars were popular at first, their concern about their own privileges and their support of indulgences and preachments against dissenters such as Wycliffe and Martin Luther lost them support. When Henry VIII shut down the friaries, John Tavener, the king's agent and musician wrote, 'The devotion of the people has clear gone'. Boston had turned Protestant.

The refectory, the only surviving part of the Blackfriars Friary is now the successful Blackfriars Theatre and Arts centre

Sculpture by Rick Kirby erected on the site of the Franciscan Friary commemorates the medieval friary and celebrates 'new life'. It was commissioned by the Longhurst Housing Association and unveiled in 1997

More Information: *The Story of Boston by Richard Gurnham; Boston, 1086-1225, A Medieval Town by Stephen H. Rigby; Boston Blackfriars, edited by WM Ormrod*

THE REBELLION OF 1536
Neil Wright

King Henry VIII came to the throne in 1509 and for most of his life was a good Catholic, being given the title of "Defender of the Faith" by the Pope. But when Henry wanted to divorce his first wife, Catherine of Aragon, the Pope would not give the necessary approval and the King took upon himself the position of head of the Church in England. Henry was not a Protestant and stayed somewhat traditional in his beliefs, but that did not stop him targeting the monasteries of England, some of which were very wealthy by that time. In the 1530s all monasteries in England were closed, the smaller ones first and the larger ones soon afterwards.

Lord Hussey (AM Cook, 1948)

Many people in England still adhered to Catholic beliefs and, while they may not have protested at the King taking the role of Supreme Head of the Church, the closure and plundering of monasteries did cause alarm among some, who feared he would also rob their parish churches and guild chapels. This concern took violent form in Yorkshire and Lincolnshire. In Yorkshire it was called the Pilgrimage of Grace whereas in this county it became known as the Lincolnshire Rising.

Trouble started in Louth on 2 October 1536, spread to Caistor and on 3 October two men were killed at Horncastle. A few thousand rebels marched to Lincoln from where they sent a letter to the King setting out six demands. As soon as the King heard of the rebellion he sent troops into the county, some led by Charles Brandon, Duke of Suffolk. Boston was divided. A large group of protestors headed for Ancaster Heath to rendezvous with the rebels, while Anthony Irby rode out of Boston with around 100 men to join Suffolk.

The uprising only lasted about a week and then many of the rebels dispersed and went home. Some rebel leaders, and a few gentlemen who had supported them, submitted to the Duke of Suffolk at Stamford on 13 October, and later many were executed.

Hussey Tower, Boston (Richard Austin)

Lord Hussey was the King's representative in Lincolnshire but instead of raising forces to put down the rebellion he sought to negotiate, but then fled from Sleaford to join some royal forces at Nottingham. For his failure to put down the rebellion, Lord Hussey was executed for treason and his property seized by the crown. This property included his mansion in Boston, approached through a gatehouse off South End, built about 1460 by Richard Benyngton collector of taxes and justice of the peace for Boston. The brick tower of the mansion survives as a ruin that can be approached from Skirbeck Road.

Meghan Markle, Duchess of Sussex is a distant relative of Lord Hussey.

No sooner had the Lincolnshire Rising been supressed another, larger rebellion broke out in the North. Known as, the Pilgrimage of Grace its banner was similar to the banner Boston vicar and historian AM Cook says was carried by the Lincolnshire Rising (courtesy of Lancaster City Museum)

More Information: *The Lincolnshire Rising 1536, by Anne Ward*

THE GUILDS (1260-1545)
David Radford

Death was a constant thought-line in medieval times. Hell was the destination of the outright wicked whilst the saints went straight to Paradise. The rest were destined to be painfully purified by fire and ice in Purgatory before being allowed into heaven. The belief was that the time spent in purgatory could be shortened by the way a person lived, along with the prayers and pious acts of their friends after they had died. This led craftsmen and merchants, in particular, to form 'religious clubs' or guilds to ensure that everyone followed honest trading practices and that others would go on praying for them after death.

The guildhall of St Mary's Guild (FL Griggs, 1914)

Medieval Boston became renowned for its religious guilds. There were about nineteen in the town functioning as trading collectives and religious societies. The earliest was the Guild of the Blessed Virgin Mary formed in 1260 by some of the town's merchants. Others came later, such as the Guild of St Simon and St Jude for mariners and the non-trade guild called 'The Fellowship of Heaven'.

For the price of a subscription, the guild provided a variety of benefits from personalised funerals to special masses. Gifts were also distributed to the poor on behalf of the members. Guilds were open to all who could afford the membership fees which varied enormously. Some such as the Corpus Christi Guild were perceived as a rich man's club with high ranking men and women, churchmen and local merchants on its books. These wealthier guilds could afford to build chapels with priests to serve in them and pay Bedesmen to say daily prayers. Bedesmen were so named after the string of beads called a Rosary that they used when praying. Members could also buy, from the Pope, special certificates called

St Mary's Guildhall Museum

indulgences which would guarantee to shorten by hundreds of days or more the time that a person would have to spend in Purgatory.

The less well-off guilds used 'chantries', small side chapels or altars, in St Botolph's or in the chapels of the wealthier guilds, where members would light candles on certain days and hold services. The Guild of St Anne claimed to have their saint's finger which, for a fee, a pilgrim could visit to get additional time off from Purgatory.

The larger guilds ran active social and business calendars, with banquets and assemblies where they would manage their affairs and conduct some of the town's business. Grand processions were held to celebrate Sundays, saints' feast days and other religious anniversaries; Guild aldermen and priests wearing stunning vestments, paraded to St Botolph's through a crowded town. It was noisy with the chanting of prayers, souvenir sellers and musicians, all accompanied by the incessant ringing of church bells.

The idea of purgatory eventually lost credibility, thanks to Martin Luther, and when Henry VIII seized all their religious property and treasures, guild life came to an abrupt end. The valuable guild assets were transferred to the newly formed Boston Corporation in 1545 and senior guild members were appointed as Aldermen, the forerunner of Councillors.

Before then some functions, such as the market and bridge maintenance, were the responsibility of the Lord of the Manor of Hallgarth, part of the Honour of Richmond and this was also passed over to the Corporation in 1545.

Each guild had its own seal for use on official documents
(i) Guild of St Mary; (ii) Guild of St Peter & Paul; (iii) Guild of Holy Trinity

(i)    *(ii)*    *(iii)*

More Information: *The Guilds in Boston by W.M. Ormrod; The History and Antiquities of Boston by Pishey Thompson; The Story of Boston by Richard Gurnham; Boston St Mary's Guildhall by John Almond & David Lambourne*

MAUD FOSTER
Ann Carlton

Boston's Maud Foster Drain runs in an almost straight line from Cowbridge to its outfall into the Witham to the east of the dock entrance. It dates from 1568 and is the oldest of Boston's main drains. It is named after Maud Foster, an early 16th century Boston woman, whose entrepreneurial achievements are as impressive as the drain that bears her name.

Maud Foster Drain where it passes Maud Foster windmill, formerly known as Reckitt's windmill.

Maud Foster drain straightened the course of the Skirbeck River so reducing the risk of flooding to the town of Boston (Chris Sidebottom)

Maude was born circa 1520 and she married Richard Foster from Skirbeck in about 1539. He was a mariner and was the co-owner of the boat *Mary-Anne*, a collier. This was probably an English 'hoy', a single-masted sailing vessel with a pair of oars at the stern that could carry about 20 tons in its hold and had a canvas structure for the crew on its deck. Records show that Robert worked the *Mary-Anne* mainly between October and March. The cargo taken north was probably stone from the monasteries that were being demolished at the time. The vessel returned south with a cargo of coal for use in houses, bake-houses and the like. Because coal was a very dirty cargo, the *Mary-Anne* used Boston's Holm Quay, near Holm Point where the Witham turned to the south-east as it made its way to the sea.

Richard died in 1568 leaving his share in the *Mary-Anne* to Maud. Under her direction the business continued to prosper, supplying coal to regular clients which included the parish of Skirbeck and the Corporation, which

Maud Foster drain and Rawson's Bridge (Chris Sidebottom)

made it available to the poor at reduced prices. Maud also developed other interests, including two shops which may have been close to the town centre.

Her astuteness as a business woman was evident when in 1568, the year of her husband's death, the Corporation proposed to reduce the risk of flooding by digging a new cut along the line of the Scire Bec as far as Cowbridge. Tradition says it was named after Maud Foster who owned the land involved and 'for which she gave consent to its passage on very favourable conditions'. Coincidentally at that time the Corporation agreed that Maud could have the two cellars, a cottage and three acres of pasture in the Holms, sometimes called Dock Pastures, at a rent fixed for her lifetime. Her business acumen was also demonstrated in her agreement with another land owner in 1574, when she used coal as surety.

At her death in November 1581, Maud's estate was worth in the region of £300, more than half-a-million pounds today. Her will, drawn up by Alderman Thorold, a future mayor of Boston, bequeathed a bushel of coal to 20 poor widows next time the *Mary-Anne* docked, £5 to "Mrs Worship", the vicar's wife, lambs to a number of friends and her best dress, trimmed with fur to her god-daughter. The *Mary-Anne* passed to Gregory Foster, and her relatives in the Hill family took over her coal store and the tenancy of the land she had rented from the Corporation some thirteen years earlier.

The Maud Foster Drain and the Maud Foster Mill (courtesy of Bryan S. Graves)

BOSTON'S ROYAL CHARTER, 1545
Neil Wright

Local government in Boston is nearly 500 years old. Boston Corporation, which preceded the present Boston Borough Council, was created by a charter issued by King Henry VIII in 1545. Before then some functions, such as the market and bridge maintenance, were the responsibility of the Lord of the Manor of Hallgarth. Others were organised by the parish. The suggestion that Boston's leading burgesses should ask the King for a charter came from Charles Brandon, Duke of Suffolk, a powerful nobleman in Lincolnshire who owned Tattershall Castle and Grimsthorpe Castle.

By the 1540s the King had acquired a large amount of property in Boston from closed monasteries, the Order of Knights of St John, three of the four friaries in the town and from Lord Hussey who had been executed for failing to put down the Lincolnshire Rising. The Duke of Richmond had just died and the Honour of Richmond with all its rights and property as owner of the Manor of Hallgarth in Boston, had reverted to Henry VIII.

The King could have appointed officials to manage his rights and property in the town, but an alternative suggested by Brandon was for the local elite to ask the King to create a Municipal Corporation with themselves as its members.

The Corporation would take on all the property and rights held by the King and could also elect two members of Parliament.

Boston Borough regalia with the mace and ceremonial oars,
(Andrew Lamming)

Borough Mayor Councillor Richard Austin BEM, one of more than 300 councillors who have served the town as Mayor of Boston since 1545

On 14th May 1545 the King granted the Charter and in return Boston paid the King £1,646 15s 4d. The Corporation consisted of a Mayor, 12 Aldermen and 18 Common Councilmen; its first members being named in the Charter. As members died or resigned the remaining members of the Corporation appointed people to fill the vacancies. The Corporation now replaced the Guilds as the main organisation in the town.

Nicholas Robertson, the first Mayor, had formerly been Alderman of St Mary's Guild, and leaders of the other Guilds also joined the Corporation. The Guilds then dissolved themselves and gave their buildings, money and other property and responsibilities to the Corporation.

Since 1546 there have been two major changes in Boston's local government. From December 1835 Councillors have been elected by eligible townspeople, and in 1974 the Corporation and the Boston Rural District Council (which from 1894 governed the surrounding area) were replaced by the Borough of Boston.

The town's heraldic shield and charter: The three coronets represent the Dukes of Richmond, Suffolk and Brittany, the major land owners in Boston at the time of Henry VIII.

The Seal of the Mayor as Admiral of the Wash (AM Cook, 1934)

Today the Mayor has a non-political role, acting as the symbolic head and first citizen of the Borough of Boston. But this has not always been the case. The Borough Mayor also has the naval rank of Admiral of the Wash. It is now ceremonial but it was once a position with real powers. When England was threatened with invasion and her ships were attacked, Queen Elizabeth I called upon her major ports to provide ships for the nation's defence. She gave the mayor of Boston the naval rank of Admiral of the Wash and the responsibility of defending the port and the Wash. Among the town's regalia are two ceremonial oar-maces, a pair of halberds and the Seal of the Admiral of the Wash bearing a merchant ship with its sail decorated with three coronets as pictured here.

Ceremonial Oar-Mace bearing Queen Elizabeth I cypher (CW Pilcher)

JOHN FOXE (1516-1587)
Patrick Corke

Bostonian John Foxe was very influential in the development of the Church of England as it is today. Queen Elizabeth I ordered that every parish church in England should have two books, The Book of Common Prayer by Cranmer and The Book of Martyrs by John Foxe. Some of the wording often used in baptisms, marriages and funerals is based on them.

John Foxe

Author Patrick Corke examining an early edition of Foxe's Book of Martyrs in St Botolph's historic library.

John Foxe's Book of Martyrs was first published in English in 1563 by John Day. Called *Acts and Monuments* it recounted in graphic detail the persecution of Protestants by the Catholic Church. Further editions appeared in 1570, 1576 and 1583. The book gave a history of Christian martyrs going back to Roman times and highlighted more recent events including the sufferings of the Lollards such as John Wycliffe and Protestant martyrs such as Cranmer, Ridley and Latimer during the reign of Queen Mary. It was a must have book for the educated Protestant. Francis Drake even took a copy on his voyage to South America in 1579.

John Foxe was born in Boston in 1516 in a house on Fish Hill where the present 'Stump & Candle' stands. After the death of his father, his mother re-married and he moved to Coningsby. He attended Tattershall College before entering Brasenose College Oxford at the age of 16 where he met Hugh Latimer and William Tyndale; both of whom were to become martyrs.

Although he resigned his College Fellowship in 1545 for religious reasons, Foxe was ordained as a deacon during the reign of Edward VI by the Bishop of London, Nicholas Ridley, who was later among the Oxford Martyrs burned at the stake on the orders of Queen Mary. John and his wife, Agnes, chose voluntary exile on the continent where they were often 'wretchedly poor'.

After Mary's death Foxe returned to England and completed his first English edition of his Book of

Foxe's birthplace on Fish Hill has undergone many alterations over the centuries (Pishey Thompson, 1856)

Martyrs. It met with popular acclaim and was read by a wide circle of people. Although Foxe received no royalties for his work, it led to instant fame. Among its pages were many memorable pictures of the most recent martyrdoms, immortalizing the words of the 68 year-old Hugh Latimer at his burning: 'Be of good courage master Ridley, and play the man. This day we shall light in England such a candle as I trust by God's grace shall never be put out'.

Foxe's book is not impartial. It tries to link the earliest Christian martyrs, persecuted by Imperial Rome, with the Protestant martyrs, persecuted by a Catholic Rome. Both he saw as enemies of the true Church. This proved influential, particularly among Puritan circles.

After Foxe's death in 1587, his book continued to be printed. The Catholic Church and others saw it in terms of Protestant propaganda. It was challenged in the 19th-century with the rise of High Anglicanism and continues to be a source of debate in universities.

More Information: 'The Acts and Monuments Online' by John Foxe, the unabridged internet version

THE PILGRIM FATHERS
Luke Skerritt

In the early 1600s a group called 'Separatists', people who wanted to worship as they wished rather than as the Church of England dictated, were meeting and worshipping God in secret. This was dangerous as they risked arrest if caught. Among their number were William Bradford, later to become governor of the Plymouth Colony in America and William Brewster. A ship was organised to take them across the North Sea to Holland where they could live in religious freedom.

Replica of the Mayflower in Plymouth Harbour, Massachusetts

Escape

In secret, one night in the autumn of 1607, this passionate and determined group of men, women and children met the ship on the edge of The Wash at Scotia Creek, Fishtoft, near Boston. They had travelled 60 miles from Scrooby, near Gainsborough, and were weary but hopeful for their new life across the sea in Holland.

Arrest

To their horror the captain of the ship had betrayed them and they were suddenly surrounded by soldiers. After rifling through their possessions and seizing money, books, clothes and other personal items, the party was carried to the town by boat where they were made a great spectacle for the crowds who had flocked to see what was happening.

Imprisonment

Without their possessions and any hope of reaching Holland, the group were brought before the magistrates at the Guildhall and held in its cells. Messengers were sent to inform the Privy Council in London what had happened. Many in Boston were sympathetic towards them so the town's magistrates treated them courteously while they waited for instructions about the charges to be brought against the group. William Bradford, who was 18 years old at the time, wrote later that 'they were fairly treated'.

The cells in the Guildhall Museum where some of the Pilgrim Fathers were held while awaiting trial

The New World

After a month's imprisonment word arrived back from the Privy Council that the majority were to be sent back 'from whence they came'. Many however, including the leaders, were eventually able to reach Leiden in Holland, where they joined others from England. In 1620 it was decided to start completely new lives in a new land. The voyage to the New World was to be long and dangerous. Of their two ships, the Speedwell, had to be abandoned, leaving the Mayflower to sail on alone. A group of 102, including many who had been imprisoned in Boston, Lincolnshire, arrived in the New World on 20 November 1620.

The name Pilgrim Fathers was not used until 1820. The phrase was coined from William Bradford who had described the Separatists he was with as having left as 'pilgrims'. The Pilgrim Monument commemorating the events of 1607 can be seen in Boston's Havenside Country Park. The cells in the Guildhall where some were held can also be visited.

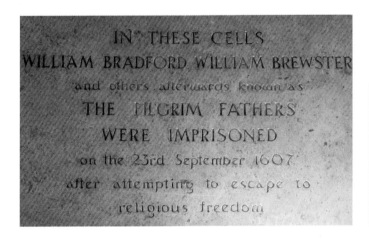

Memorial to the Pilgrim Fathers in Havenside Country Park

More Information: *Tales of the Guildhall by Andrew Malkin with Luke Skerritt & Polly Wilkinson; One Small Candle: The Story of William Bradford and the Pilgrim Fathers by Mrs Evelyn Tidman*

REVEREND JOHN COTTON
(1585-1652)
Barry Cotton

Reverend John Cotton is perhaps one of the best-known personalities to have lived in Boston, Lincolnshire. He served as the town's vicar from 1612 until 1633. Cotton then became a mentor and a guide to America's Founding Fathers after fleeing arrest in England for being Puritan. He helped in founding Boston, Massachusetts, established the first public school in North America when he created the Boston Latin School in 1635 and played a pivotal role in the founding of Harvard, America's first university.

John Cotton was born in Derby on 4 December 1585. At the age of 13 he entered Trinity College, Cambridge and received his MA in 1606. Eight years later he was a Fellow of Emmanuel College, Cambridge and soon a distinguished university lecturer and Dean, fluent in Latin, Greek and Hebrew. In 1612, he was offered the position of Vicar of Boston by the Corporation. At that time the Bishop of Lincoln thought him 'young and unfit to be over such a fractious people imbued with the Puritan spirit'. But John, abandoning his promising academic career, embraced the call to church ministry with enthusiasm.

Revd John Cotton

Although he lacked pastoral experience, in his first full year as vicar he conducted over sixty baptisms, thirty marriages and one hundred burials, becoming respected and well-loved by his parishioners. He also found time that first year to gain his Bachelor of Divinity degree and began to embrace the Puritan principles that would be the hallmark of his life. Within a few years he started to abandon such practices as genuflection and the wearing of surplices at St Botolph's, in direct contradiction to the church rituals being promoted by King Charles I and his leading churchman, William Laud.

In 1630, 21 of his congregation led by Thomas Dudley, Isaac Johnson, and Simon Bradstreet joined others migrating to New England. Cotton travelled to Southampton to see off the flotilla that included the *Arabella* as its flagship. Before the fleet sailed, Cotton preached one of his best-remembered sermons - 'God's Promise

John Cotton Memorial,
Pemberton Square, Boston MA

The John Cotton stained glass window, St Botolph's Church, Boston, Lincolnshire

to His Plantation'. When William Laud became Archbishop of Canterbury in 1633, Cotton's position became untenable. He went into hiding, resigned as vicar and sailed for New England in the *Griffin* with four other families from his congregation. More than 166 from the Boston area eventually left the town for a new life in America.

John Cotton lived for nineteen years in Boston, Massachusetts surrounded by members of his Boston, Lincolnshire congregation who played key roles in governing Massachusetts. Four of them: Thomas Dudley, Richard Bellingham, John Leverett and Simon Bradstreet served as governors and deputy governors of the Massachusetts Bay Colony.

After his death in 1652, Cotton became known as the Puritan Patriarch of New England.

The John Cotton pulpit is named after Revd John Cotton who regularly preached from it while vicar of St Botolph's Church.

More Information: *The Career of John Cotton: Puritanism and the American Experience by Larzer Ziff*
John Cotton: An Intimate Investigation of his Life and Times by Barry Cotton

BOSTON AND THE FOUNDING OF MASSACHUSETTS
Barry Cotton

The pivotal role that Boston, Lincolnshire, played in the founding of Boston, Massachusetts, has yet to be fully recognized on either side of the Atlantic. During years of the Puritan Great Migration approximately 20,000 immigrants sailed from England to The New World. Included in this number were 166 people from the Boston, Lincolnshire area. Four of these Richard Bellingham, Simon Bradstreet, Thomas Dudley and John Leverett, became governor or deputy governor for all but four years of the Massachusetts Bay Colony's first fifty-eight years of existence.

In April 1630 a fleet of 11 ships, commonly called the Winthrop Fleet after its leader John Winthrop, arrived at Salem. America. This settlement had been established several years earlier. Among the first colonists were Edmund Ingalls, his wife and their five children from Skirbeck. The Rev Samuel Skelton with his wife and their three children, from Tattershall arrived in a later migration. Rev Skelton had served as chaplain to the Earl of Lincoln, a known supporter of the new colonists.

In 1629 the New England Company which had its America base in Salem was restructured and the Massachusetts Bay Company was formed. It obtained a new Royal Charter and, at a shareholders meeting later that year, it was proposed to move the new company from London to the New World. John Winthrop was elected governor.

Plaque in St Botolph's Church commemorating the five men from Boston, Lincolnshire who became governors of Boston, Massachusetts.

Many began investing in the company, including ten men from Boston. They sent Thomas Coney, Boston's town clerk, to submit their request

Founders' Memorial, Boston MA

Boston, MA (David Mark on Pixabay)

to purchase £25 stock each. They included Atherton Hough, Boston's mayor, Richard Bellingham, Boston's MP, Simon Bradstreet, Thomas Dudley, Thomas Leverett, William Coddington, Charles Fiennes (brother to the Earl of Lincoln), Herbert Pelham, Abraham Mellows and Isaac Johnson.

Although each eventually sailed to New England, only six actually accompanied Winthrop to Salem in 1630. Among them were Isaac Johnson, the chief financier of the Massachusetts Bay Company, and his wife, Lady Arabella, sister to the Earl of Lincoln. The flagship of the Winthrop Fleet was named *The Arbella* in her honour. Sadly not long after arriving in Salem, Lady Arabella died of scurvy.

While Salem was their initial destination they soon realized a more plentiful supply of fresh water would be needed for the growing numbers. Isaac Johnson's friend and former college roommate, William Blaxton from Horncastle, who had sailed to New England with Robert Gorges in 1623, had settled on the Shawmut Peninsula in 1625. Knowing that the peninsula could provide plenty of water, Blaxton invited Isaac Johnson and the newly arrived colonists to settle Shawmut. Trimountaine, as the area was originally known, was renamed Boston on 7 September 1630, after the Lincolnshire town many of them had left.

Ironically, Isaac Johnson died twenty-three days later, but the colony he helped create did not look back. It grew rapidly and by 1720 was the largest city in the colony, with a population of 12,000. New York's population at that time was about 7,000.

More Information: *Boston: Its Story & People, George Bagley; History and Antiquities of Boston by Pishey Thompson; The Memorial History of Boston Vol. I-III, Justin Winsor; Transcription of Minutes of the Corporation of Boston: Vol II (1608-1638) by John F. Bailey; The Parish Registers of Boston in the County of Lincoln by Frank Besant*

ANNE HUTCHINSON (1591-1643)
Eve LaPlante

Anne Marbury Hutchinson who was born in Alford in 1591, first came to Boston when she was in her early twenties to hear the Rev John Cotton preach. She made many further visits over the next twenty years, often with her husband and children. Already admired for her Biblical teaching and her skill as a midwife, she became part of Cotton's inner circle of believers where she gained a public voice; something that no woman of her day could expect to have. Cotton said of her: "Mistress Hutchinson had more [people] resort to her for counsel about matters of conscience, and clearing up men's spiritual estates, than any minister."

In 1634, she and her large family followed Cotton to the New World where she joined his congregation and collaborated with him by running Scripture meetings in her home while he preached their shared theology at church. By

1636, her meetings were attracting large numbers of prominent men and women eager for social reform. However, many others began to feel threatened by her growing influence. In 1637 she was put on trial for her theological views and for stepping outside the bounds assigned to women, being charged by the governor John Winthrop with heresy and sedition.

At her trial the 46 year-old defended herself brilliantly, using Scripture to support her right to teach men and to preach in public, something colonial law barred women from doing. Cotton, who had long defended her rights, realizing that she would be convicted, abandoned her to save himself. The judges ordered that she should be banished for behaving in a manner "not fitting for [her] sex."

Exiled, Anne and her family and followers moved to Rhode Island where she created a settlement

Anne Hutchinson statue

Self portrait of a woman of Dutch descent, contemporary with Anne Hutchinson (Eve LaPlante)

dedicated to freedom of worship and speech. She became the only woman to co-found (with Roger Williams) an American colony. Her final move was to modern day New York where in 1642, after her husband's death, she and her young family settled in the Bronx among the Dutch. A year later she and six of her children were mistaken for a Dutch family and killed in a Native American raid.

While most seventeenth-century women's experiences are lost to us, Hutchinson persists as a stirring example of one who spoke her mind despite the consequences. In a time when women were not allowed to vote, speak in public, teach outside their home, or sign a legal document, Hutchinson stood up for her right to express her own beliefs and her fundamental equality with men. Her commitment to free speech and religious liberty inspired the Portsmouth Compact of 1638, one source of the religious-freedom clause in the U.S. Constitution's Bill of Rights. The seeds of the ongoing struggle for women's and human rights can be found in the dramatic story of this American founding mother.

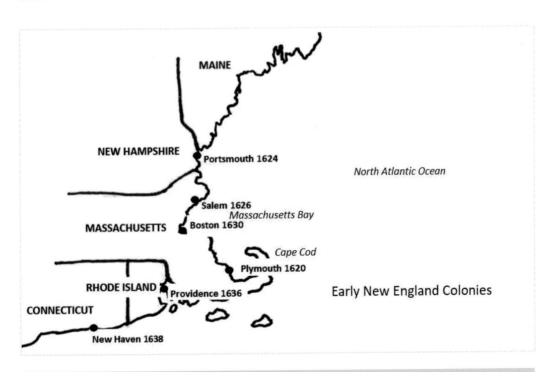

Early New England Colonies

MAINE

NEW HAMPSHIRE

Portsmouth 1624

North Atlantic Ocean

Salem 1626

Massachusetts Bay

MASSACHUSETTS   Boston 1630

Cape Cod

Plymouth 1620

RHODE ISLAND   Providence 1636

CONNECTICUT

New Haven 1638

More Information: *The Uncommon Life of Anne Hutchinson, the Woman Who Defied the Puritans by Eve LaPlante*

BOSTON AND THE CIVIL WAR
Ian Middleton

The crowning of Charles 1 in 1625 proved to be a traumatic turning point for Boston. No other town in the country was more committed to Parliamentarianism or Puritanism. A series of events in the 1630s only strengthened Boston's resolve against their king. This included the enforcement of liturgical forms of worship opposed by the Puritans and the imposition of a controversial tax called Ship-Money in 1635. Although the town clerk, Thomas Coney, successfully petitioned the Privy Council for a reduction, little tax was collected. Charles also tried to raise troops from Boston's trained men to help put down the Scottish rebellion, but the town resisted all attempts as they were in sympathy with Scotland's opposition to the King.

When the King's continued overbearing demands finally edged the country into civil war, Boston was already a Parliamentarian stronghold. In August 1642 its forces arrested a group of royalist officers who had landed at Skegness from the Netherlands. Infuriated, Charles issued warrants forbidding other Lincolnshire towns to assist them but Lord Lindsey, the King's general, hesitated to attack the town as he knew it could raise 4,000 men within six hours notice.

Parliamentarian Sir Anthony Irby, Boston's MP, raised a company of dragoons that fought at the Battle of Edgehill, 1642 among others (AM Cook, 1948)

This front page of a propaganda pamphlet carried news of the capture of ten Royalists at Skegness by men from Boston

In December Sir Anthony Irby, Boston's MP, rode north with his dragoons to join Parliament's army that was trying to stop the Earl of Newcastle's Royalist forces advancing south. They failed and eventually Newcastle captured the town of Newark, and several important Lincolnshire towns. Boston was now virtually surrounded so Newcastle had Boston in his sights. His forces had taken Tattershall Castle and he fortified Bolingbroke Castle and Wainfleet. Spalding had been captured by troops from Crowland and reports reached the town saying the Royalists had reached Swineshead.

The Corporation purchased cannon for the town's defence and earth banks were probably built along the

These cannon on display in the Guildhall Museum were purchased from King's Lynn for the defence of the town

Statue of Oliver Cromwell outside the Houses of Parliament, London (Ron Porter on Pixabay)

Damage purported to be caused by Parliamentarians firing their weapons during their occupation of the Stump (Chris Sidebottom)

Barditch. In June 1643 Parliament sent 400 muskets to reinforce the town. Oliver Cromwell, who commanded the cavalry in the town, stayed at the Three Tuns in the Market Place. His cavalry horses were tethered to the pillars in the Stump. His troops did a lot of damage to the inside of the church. The marks left by firing muskets at the walls can still be seen.

To Boston's surprise, Newcastle did not attack but left to lay siege to Hull. On 9th October 1643 the Parliamentarian Eastern Association Army led by the Earl of Manchester marched out of the town to start retaking Lincolnshire. While engaged in laying siege to Bolingbroke Castle news of an approaching Royalist force meant that Oliver Cromwell and his cavalry immediately raced off towards Winceby. The next morning, 11 October 1643, the Royalists were taken by surprise and overwhelmed within half an hour when Cromwell attacked them at Winceby. The Civil War continued to ebb and flow but Boston held firm; an important Parliamentarian town to the end.

More Information: Boston and the Great Civil War by A.A. Garner

WILLIAM STUKELEY (1697-1765)
David Haycock

Dr. William Stukeley was one of the founders of modern field archaeology and one of the 18th-century's distinguished antiquarians. He was born in Holbeach in 1697 and after studying medicine at Corpus Christi, Cambridge and a brief stint in London studying anatomy, he set up his practice in Boston. While living in the town from 1710 to 1717 he played an active part in its life. He established a botanical club, became a trustee of the new Blue Coat School and was a member of the recently founded Spalding Gentleman's Society that is still in existence today. In 1713, Dr. Stukeley was honored by being made a freeman of Boston.

William Stukeley

During his time in Boston that he began making his annual tour of England, accounts of which he published in 1724 as *Itinerarium curiosum, or, An account of the antiquitys and remarkable curiositys in nature or art, observ'd in travels thro' Great Brittan, illustrated with copper prints.* A keen amateur artist, he made drawings of what he observed, including a view of St Botolph's church. He complained to a friend of the 'dirty roads and dull company' he had experienced during his time in Lincolnshire and he decided to move back to London. There, with others he re-founded the Society of Antiquaries and that same year, 1718, was elected a Fellow of the Royal Society. It was here he became friends with Sir Isaac Newton and would go on to write one of the first biographical accounts of his life.

Stukeley now began a scientific study of Stonehenge and Avebury in Wiltshire where he studied, measured and drew the monuments in great detail. His methods and practices laid down the principles for modern archaeology. His historical and religious interpretation led him to conclude that these ancient monuments were the work of ancient British Druids, based upon ideas first advanced by John Aubrey a century earlier. He published two significant books: Stonehenge: A Temple Restor'd to the British Druids (1740) and Avebury: A Temple of the British Druids (1743). Together they fixed in the public mind the concept that the Druids were the builders of these ancient works.

By the date of their publication Stukeley had again abandoned London in favour of a return to Lincolnshire. In 1726 he moved to Grantham,

St Botolph's - a drawing by Stukeley
©Trustees of the British Museum.

practicing first as a physician before being ordained in the Church of England, taking up the living of All Saints, Stamford in 1730. He returned to London as vicar of St George the Martyr in Queen Square, Bloomsbury in 1747, where he remained until his death in 1765. In his later years he was increasingly seen as an eccentric figure, obsessed with Druids, ancient coins, theology and the distant past.

Drawing of Stonehenge by Stukeley

More Information: *William Stukeley: Science, Archaeology and Religion in Eighteenth-Century England by David Boyd Haycock*

TURNPIKE ROADS
Neil Wright

In the middle of the 18th century Turnpike Trusts took over the maintenance and improvement of the main roads leading to the town and created a transport revolution. Before then each parish was responsible for looking after its own roads and through routes, that had heavy usage, received a little more attention than the other roads solely used by local people. To improve the quality of main through routes, Turnpike Trusts were created by act of Parliament to take over the longer stretches of road between towns and through many parishes. They were financed by charging tolls on those who used the roads.

The first road to be 'turnpiked' in the area was from Boston through Swineshead and to Donington. This linked to other turnpiked roads thus connecting Boston to the great North Road at Norman Cross. The Donington Turnpike was authorised in 1758. A raised causeway called a Rampar was built to avoid flooding where it crossed the southern part of Holland Fen. That Rampar is still part of the main A52 road today and often referred to by many locals as the 'Swineshead Rampar'. That trust created a side road from the Rampar to Langrick Ferry which passed a natural source of gravel at Amber Hill that could be used for road maintenance.

The turnpike barring the road to Wainfleet at Burton Corner, Boston, before its demolition in 1875 (Boston Guardian, 1938)

A turnpike marker in the pavement outside Cammack's furniture store

Stage coaches continue to use the turnpikes long after the companies were abolished, as shown in this picture of a coach and its passengers outside the Ram Hotel, Wide Bargate (Neil Watson Collection)

Milestone half-buried in the bank opposite the Pincushion on the old road to Spalding.

On Turnpike roads every mile was marked by a milestone like this 'Boston 2 miles' on the A52 at the junction with Wortley's Lane.

The Donington Trust also took over London Road from Boston as far as Bicker Haven. They evidently thought the road across Bicker Haven itself too difficult to take on. In 1764 another trust took over the road from Spalding to Donnington and turnpiked the road from Gosberton through Bicker Haven to completing the turn-piking of the whole main road from Boston to Spalding.

In 1765 another trust was formed for the road between Boston and Alford. It entered Boston via Spilsby Road. Turnpike trusts did not usually cover roads in towns but this Trust's duties extended as far as a metal marker in Wide Bargate; this marker still survives in the pavement in front of Cammack's shop. People might try to avoid paying tolls on this road by cutting across the West Fen to get into Boston by a different route so this Trust also took over Horncastle Road alongside the Maud Foster drain and erected a toll bar at Cowbridge. After the railways were opened to Boston in 1848 road traffic declined, Turnpike Trusts had less money and they were abolished in the 1870s.

PROSPERITY AND PLEASURE
Sharon Middleton

Boston, from around 1760 to about 1860, was in an economic boom. By 1826 it was one of the three leading corn markets in the country and by 1837 it was the largest town in the county. The improvement to its financial status was in part due to the successful drainage of the fens that released huge tracts of highly fertile land, and to improvement in communications which opened up new markets for the crops grown. Roads that had been tracks became turnpikes, and in 1848 the first railway line reached Boston. The port was busy shipping huge quantities of crops to London and beyond.

The 1840s and 1850s saw a diversification from agrarian occupations into engineering and manufacturing. Engineering firms such as Tuxfords, exploited their farming knowledge to develop steam-driven farm machinery. Ship building, flour milling and featherbed manufacture became important.

The extra wealth led to many public and private projects. Among them was the Corporation Buildings, a fish market with dwellings above,

The opening of Fydell Crescent in 1879 was marked by an extravagant day of events (The Pictorial World)

built between 1769 and 1772 in the Market Place. William Marrat wrote in 1814 that it was a fine building 'but the stench which it sends forth in summer time, is extremely disagreeable'. The Assembly Rooms replaced the unfashionable Butter Cross and by 1842 the town also had a new Sessions House (court).

Leisure activities in Boston included balls, theatre productions by the Robertson Theatre Company from Lincoln's Theatre Royal during January and February, and the prevailing trend of 'bathing'. Boston had its own bathing-house and Skirbeck, two. One opened in 1820 and the more sophisticated one in South End opened in 1834. This offered hot, cold and tepid options. Sea bathing was also popular from around 1800. Freiston Shore, Boston's coastal playground, had two hotels, Plummer's Hotel that still exists today, and the Anchor Inn.

The town also had its own pleasure garden, 'The People's Park', modelled on London's famous Vauxhall Gardens. The Stamford Mercury described a Gala held there on 12 June 1816 as being 'illuminated with 3,000 lamps'. The entertainment included 'dancing, fire-balloons, and pyrotechnic exhibitions, all of which went off with the greatest éclat'.

Frieston Shore was Boston's coastal playground, a popular destination for day trippers and holiday makers as shown in this picture of carriages outside the Marine Hotel in 1900 (courtesy of Richard Starbuck)

With all this prosperity, shopping fast became a leisure pursuit. Shops not only sold everyday essentials but all manner of luxury items. In 1781, J. Noble was offering wallpaper 'in the French style' with a 25% discount. The Corporation built the UKs first shopping parade in the Market Place in 1820, with access to the flats above the shops located at the rear. In 1822 the Pygot & Co's trade directory shows there were 393 shops in Boston, however, its 1835 directory lists 910 shops. That's a lot of shopping! John Oldrid opened his drapery store in Straight Bargate in 1804. Still occupying its original site, today's Oldrid's is Boston's largest department store.

Strait Bargate, 1910 (courtesy of Richard Starbuck)

More Information: *A Pictorial History of Boston & Boston a History and Celebration by Neil Wright; Boston Through Time by Helen Shinn.*

CAPABILITY BROWN (1716-1783)
David Radford

Capability Brown became famous in the eighteenth century for creating landscapes, lakes and great water features for the wealthy gentry on their country estates. He came to the Boston area as a young man, married a local girl and honed his engineering and water management skills.

Lancelot 'Capability' Brown was baptised on 30 August 1716 at St Winifred's, Kirkharle, a small parish in Northumberland. He went to school in Cambo, a three-mile walk across the estate of Sir William Lorraine where his father worked as land agent and his mother as a chambermaid. During these walks he observed the improvements being made to the estate as an apprentice gardener.

Sir William was an MP and a member of the Royal Society with a network of influential friends. In an age where societal snobbery seems to have been excluded from the pursuit of knowledge and its practical application, Brown's name as someone who understood how to

Capability Brown

improve an estate aesthetically and commercially must have come up in many of Sir William's conversations. Lancelot Brown's oft repeated phase 'it has great capabilities' gained him his nickname.

Capability Brown's daughter Bridget was said to be similar in appearance to her mother who she was named after

Brown came to Boston around 1738. The Deeping Fen Act of that year had authorised new drainage works between the Witham and the Glen under the direction of John Grundy. It is thought the 23-year-old was responding to the call for 'engineers' as much of Capability Brown's life-story has to be conjectured from his work and who he associated with. While we cannot be certain he worked on the Surfleet reservoir and sluice scheme he was certainly an acquaintance of both John Grundy and his son John Grundy Jnr. He was familiar with their methods.

Around this time he also met Joseph Banks, of Revesby Abbey, an MP and member of the Royal Academy. He introduced Brown to the Duke of Ancaster at Grimsthorpe Castle. There Lancelot constructed one of his earliest 'naturalised' lakes in the landscape he created. John Grundy Jnr succeeded him at Grimsthorpe, further developing Brown's vision and may later have collaborated with Brown on the feature dam and sluice disguised as a multi-arched bridge.

The landscaping the Duke of Ancaster's Grimsthrope estate was one of Lancelot Brown's early projects in Lincolnshire

While working at Grimsthorpe, Brown was called upon to repair some dams on Lord Cobham's Stowe estate which had been damaged by the severe winters of 1739 and 1740. The following year he became assistant head gardener to William Kent, the leading landscape garden designer of his day and in 1742 he succeeded him as head gardener.

The garden landscape he created at Stowe was opened to the public in 1744. In November of that year Capability married Bridget Wayet, the Boston girl with whom he had fallen in love. She was the daughter of William Wayet, a respected Boston businessman.

In July 1764 Brown received his highest accolade, a royal warrant as 'Surveyor to His Majesty's Gardens and Waters at Hampton Court'. By his death in 1783 he had completed and influenced more than 250 projects, many now being viewed as being the quintessential English countryside. The epitaph on his tomb reads: "He sought an image of Heaven".

More Information: *Capability Brown, Moving Heaven by Steffie Shields*
Capability Brown and his landscape gardens by Sarah Rutherford
Our great 'Capability' Brown landscapes, The National Trust

SIR JOSEPH BANKS (1743-1820)
Sharon Middleton

Sir Joseph Banks was one of the most influential Englishmen of his time. A companion of Captain James Cook, a friend of George III and President of the Royal Society, he was a respected botanist, explorer and naturalist who was involved in nearly all the significant scientific initiatives and voyages of explorations of the time. His name is linked to many discoveries including the genus Banksia, which he identified in Botany Bay with the help of his friend, Swedish scientist Dr Daniel Solander, and also with the introduction of the eucalyptus and acacias to the Western world. The Banks Islands named after him are a group of volcanic islands near Vanuatu in the Pacific Ocean and in Australia. There is a place called Revesby in New South Wales and one called Boston in South Australia.

Portrait of Sir Joseph Banks by Thomas Phillips, RA, painted for the Corporation of Boston and now hanging in the town's Guildhall Museum (used by permission)

Born in London in 1743 and educated at Harrow and Eton before attending Oxford University. Banks was a dedicated student, particularly of botany and entomology. In 1764, at the age of 21, when his father died, he inherited Revesby Abbey along with a large fortune. In 1766, he made his first voyage of exploration to Newfoundland and Labrador, returning home in 1768 as an experienced natural history collector and the creator of the first scientifically categorised collection of specimens.

Elected as a Fellow of the Royal Society, Banks next headed the team of botanists and artists on Captain James Cook's voyage of 1768-1771 to observe the transit of Venus in Tahiti and to explore the uncharted lands of the South Pacific. This time Banks returned with the first natural history collection of specimens from the South Seas and Australia to be

Banksias, one of the many Australian plants named after Sir Joseph Banks (Mary Findell)

seen in Britain. Boston honoured him for his "pursuit towards the increase of natural knowledge and for the discovery of new countries so beneficial to the commercial interests of these kingdoms" by making him a freeman of the Borough.

In 1772 he went on an expedition to Iceland with Dr Solander and after his return, Banks became a sought after advisor to expeditions, taking particular interest in the young Captain Matthew Flinders from Donington. In 1778 he became President of the Royal Society and in 1781 he was made a baronet. The 'Conversaziones' funded out of his personal fortune gave Fellows of the Royal Society an opportunity to demonstrate their research and it is now the Royal Society's public Summer Exhibition.

Sir Joseph continued to divide his time between his London home and Revesby where he tried, but failed to introduce a kangaroo colony. The parkland he landscaped contains many examples of the plants and trees he brought back from his explorations. Active in the local politics of Lincolnshire as well as in the navigation, drainage, surveying and accurate mapping of the county, Sir Joseph was a local magistrate and in 1819 was awarded the largely honorary title of 'Recorder' for Boston, the town's senior magistrate or judge in the local courts. Sir Joseph died in 1820.

Australian five-dollar note featuring Sir Jospeh Banks

More Information: *The Sir Joseph Banks Society Visitors Centre, 7-13 Bridge Street, Horncastle LN9 5HZ*

THE GRAND SLUICE
Richard Austin

Much of the Boston that we see today stems from the building of the Grand Sluice on the River Witham. It was built to enable easy and reliable navigation between Boston and Lincoln and to help with the drainage of large areas of fen. This heralded a new era of prosperity for Boston and many of the fine buildings we have today date back to this time. It also enabled the town to become the first in Lincolnshire to be industrialised and grow to be the largest in the County.

The Grand Sluice was built in a field north of the old town. A completely new and straight course was then dug for the Witham after it was constructed (Steve Johnston)

At high tide the sluice prevents salt water travelling upstream (Jaimaneul Freire)

The River Witham rises near the village of South Witham close to the border with Rutland then flows through Grantham, before reaching Lincoln. After passing through Lincoln's Brayford Pool and under the city's High Bridge, it continues its way to the sea. Lincoln's High Bridge was built in 1160 and is the oldest bridge in the UK with a building on it.

After Lincoln, the river passes Bardney and Kirkstead, sites of important medieval monasteries, before flowing towards Boston and through the Grand Sluice. From there it passes Boston's famous Stump and through Boston's Haven finally reaching the Wash. The total length of the river is 82 miles (132km). The important section from Lincoln High Bridge to the Grand Sluice is 31 miles long, with the fall in water level usually only about 4.5m. Before the Grand Sluice was built commercial navigation between Lincoln and

Boston had become all but impossible as the Witham meandered, silted up and even changed its course from time to time.

Construction of the Grand Sluice began in 1764 and whilst this work was being carried out the Witham was straightened out and confined between the high banks we see today. Work on the Sluice began in the middle of a field and a totally new course for the Witham was cut ready for the opening in 1766. The Sluice consists of three channels each 5.2 m wide fitted with mitre gates on both sides. Three engineers were involved: John Grundy, Langley Edwards and John Smeaton. Edwards designed the actual Sluice and was appointed as project engineer.

The Sluice controls the water levels for the 21 miles upstream to Bardney Lock. Its construction and the accompanying river improvement enabled 111,000 acres of land in the Holland, Wildmore, East and West Fens and the Lincoln Fens to be drained; then enclosed into fields for growing crops. As a result, large quantities of grain and other produce were grown, shipped to London or the new industrialised areas of the North.

The Grand Sluice showing sluice gates and the adjoining lock gate for river traffic (Shirley Rogers)

A watercolour of the Grand Sluice before the building of the railway bridge.

More Information: *Georgian Boston by Neil Wright*

THE WITHAM: BOSTON TO LINCOLN
Neil Wright

By medieval times Boston was the best place to construct a bridge over the river Witham before it entered the Wash; hence that is the reason for its location. This also made it the best port on the river for sea-going vessels. By this time Lincoln had become a major English city with the Witham connecting it to the sea and Boston serving as its outport. Wool from the monasteries in Yorkshire and the Midlands could also reach Boston via the rivers Ouse and Trent, the Fossdyke canal and the Witham. However by the 18th century the lower reaches of the river through the Fens to the north of Boston had silted up and boats could only navigate it when there was sufficient water. It has been described as a failed river. In addition it frequently over-spilled its banks causing extensive inland flooding.

This problem was solved between 1764 and 1766 when a new 12 mile long channel was cut through the Fens, abandoning the old route, and the Grand Sluice was built just north of the town. The Sluice held back the fresh water so that the channel was deep enough for boats at any time whilst at the same time it kept out the tidal waters to prevent inland flooding from the sea. The new river channel was dug in three straight sections; this was a massive engineering project. Land owners were greatly concerned that they did not loose out to the scheme, so the line of the new cut was drawn to avoid this problem.

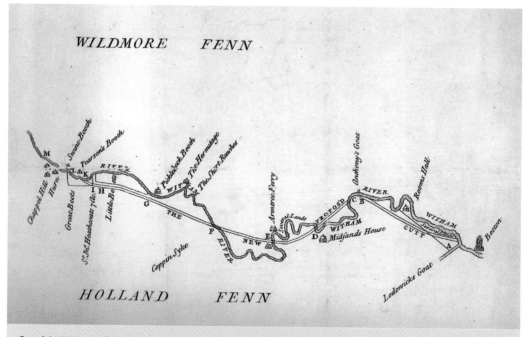

Grundy's 1753 map of the River Witham from Boston to Lincoln showing its proposed new course

Leisure craft moored along the banks of the River Witham near the Grand Sluice (courtesy of Richard Starbuck)

The new channel above Boston had high banks so the Fens on each side were protected against flooding. The Fens had been vast areas of unfenced common land subject to frequent flooding but now could be drained and divided into enclosed fields. The 22,000 acres West of Boston known as Holland Fen were enclosed in the 1770s.The East, West and Wildmore Fens totalling 40,000 acres to the north of the town were similarly dealt with between 1802 and 1812. The enclosure of the Fens was Boston's contribution to the agricultural revolution.

There was some violent opposition to the drainage and enclosure of Holland Fen but the reclamation of the three northern Fens was peaceful. Cole seed, now known as oil seed rape, was often used as the first or "pioneer" crop before cereals were grown. Oats were usually the first of the cereals to be drilled; wheat later.

The old Fens had been used for grazing large numbers of cattle as well as horses and geese. Cattle had been herded south on the hoof to feed London but cereals were now moved by ship. This led to the revival of the port and Boston's second great period of prosperity. Boston came to supply about a quarter of London's need for cereals and helped to feed the industrial revolution in the growing northern cities.

Evening sun on the Witham at Anton's Gowt (Chris Sidebottom)

BOSTON INDUSTRIALISED
Neil Wright

In the early 19th century Lincolnshire started to see changes that the industrial revolution brought to this country and Boston became the first town in the County to be industrialised. The main occupation then, as now, was agriculture and large industrial concerns in Boston arose to design implements and machines to make the growing of crops more labour efficient. Some of these machines went on to transform agriculture across the world.

Boston's industrial skyline (Neil Watson Collection)

There had been blacksmiths, wheelwrights and other ironworkers in the county for centuries and as the 19th century progressed some workshops started to grow into large engineering works. In 1803 William Howden started the Grand Sluice Ironworks at the inland port of Witham Town adjacent to the Sluice; this was the first in Boston. By 1827 he had made the first steam engines to be produced in Lincolnshire and they were used on river craft trading between Boston and Lincoln.

William Wedd Tuxford built a windmill at Mount Bridge, just outside Boston, in about 1822. He invented a machine to clean the wheat before it was milled, which he patented about 1830. Other millers wanted this machine so he set up a workshop beside his mill and when his sons joined him at the end of the decade, it developed into the Boston and Skirbeck Ironworks.

Tuxford and Sons produced the successful conception of the threshing drum which transformed agriculture round the world. These impressive machines were powered by a separate steam engine connected to it with a driving belt. The first ones were pulled by horses from farm to farm but later Tuxfords were involved in developing the steam traction engine. Such threshing sets, pulled by these traction engines were in use until the 1950s. Tuxfords' products were exported worldwide, including

Tuxford & Sons threshing machine, 1855 (The Illustrated London News)

Tuxford's Skirbeck Iron Works and its eight-sail windmill. The windmill was taken down and rebuilt in Heckington where it can still be seen (The Illustrated London News)

to France, Russia, and Australia. Examples of their machines can still be seen in museums in Edinburgh, Paris and in Sweden.

Other industries in Boston included the processing of feathers and water filters made by George Cheavin. Several firms made snuff and then cigars, the last works closing in the 1920s. Shoe Laces were made by Arthur Whittle & Co until the 1970's. There were windmills in Boston town, all but one now gone, and also breweries and tanneries.

John Fisher invented a strong form of luggage label, important as the railways made it easier for more people to travel long distances. His business flourished for over a century. At the end of the 19th century there were large steam mills that crushed imported seeds to produce oil cake for cattle feed and in the first half of the 20th century several factories were canning locally grown vegetables.

Cigar making at Whittle & Cope's, Norfolk Street , 1900 (courtesy of Neil Wright)

Shoe and boot laces were manufactured in Boston until the 1970s (Neil Watson Collection)

BANKING IN BOSTON
Sharon Middleton

The boom in banking in the UK started around 1750 when wealthy traders saw a gap in the market for lending money to others, for a price of course! These privately owned banks relied heavily on trust within the local community. Many bankers became actively involved in politics and philanthropy. At this time Boston was a wealthy town of commercial importance. The British Banking History Society records that in 1805 Boston had six banks for its 7,000 population in comparison to Exeter which had seven banks to serve its larger population of 18,000.

Boston's first bank, and the first one in Lincolnshire, was established in 1754 by William Garfit, a corn merchant and shipper at 116 High Street. In 1774 he took Bartholomew Claypon into partnership. Bartholomew's father died in 1758 leaving an estate worth £3,818, a colossal sum at that time which indicates just how wealthy some of these merchants were. In 1783 Henry Gee and Henry Clark, brewers and public house owners, founded their bank, Gee & Clark.

While both Garfit & Claypon and Gee & Clark survived the economic upheavals of the 1800s the other four banks did not. Abraham Sheath's bank, founded in 1789 was one Boston's largest banks. It failed due to over-speculation, its size offering no protection against economic depression.

William Garfit, MP

116 High Street, Boston, location of William Garfit's first bank (Chris Sidebottom)

The failure of Samuel Barnard's bank, founded around 1790, was probably due to his own excesses. Edward Wilford's bank was another casualty that year, although his bankruptcy did not prevent Wilford becoming mayor in 1823. William Ingelow's bank failed in the 1820s barely 20 years after it opened. William was father of poet Jean Ingelow.

Throughout the 19th-century the town's two remaining banks, though rivals, continued to hold a dominant positon in the town in face of competition from the newly formed joint stock banks: the Stamford, Spalding & Boston

English Banks were once allowed to issue their own bank notes. This picture is of a ten pound note issued by William Ingelow's Bank. (courtesy of Sharon Middleton)

Joint Stock Banking Co. and a branch of the National Provincial Bank. One of the first branches of the TSB was established in Boston in 1817. In 1864 Gee & Clark moved into new premises that later became home to the Midland Bank and then HSBC, until 2012. Garfit's bank also moved into new premises that same year, the building now occupied by Lloyds Bank in the Market Place.

The economic depressions of the 1870s and the greater financial power and security of the joint stock banks brought about the end of the private banks. Gee & Clarke was taken over by the Lincoln & Lindsey Bank which merged with the Midland Bank in 1913. Garfit's bank merged with Capital & Counties in 1891, with William Garfit as a director and then as its chairman in 1915. When Capital & Counties merged with Lloyds in 1918, William became a director of Lloyds. The 20th-century brought further changes eventually leaving the UK with just national banks by 1934.

Lloyds Bank in Boston's Market Place, was built in 1864 as the new premises for William Garfit's bank (Chris Sidebottom)

Barclay's Bank was built for the Stamford and Spalding Banking Company in 1876 (Chris Sidebottom)

More Information: *Banking in Boston by S.N. Davis*

THE STRAIGHTENING OF THE HAVEN
Richard Austin

The Haven is the stretch of the Witham between the Grand Sluice and the outfall to the sea. As its name implies it was a place of safety for shipping.

By 1800 The Haven between Skirbeck Church and the Wash had become wide and split into many tortuous channels. Silt and sand had accumulated over time and Boston had become almost unusable as a port. This deterioration of the river outfall also led to greater flooding problems inland.

Boston Corporation commissioned the engineer, John Rennie to survey the Haven and to draw up plans to create the deepest and straightest possible channel for the 13.5 miles from the Black Sluice to the Wash.

The mouth of the Witham showing details of its older course and its outfall into the Wash

Three Ruston Steam Excavators at work cutting the new channel for the River Witham (courtesy of Alison Austin)

He determined that one option was to straighten and shorten the channel between Skirbeck Church and Hobhole and then make a new cut from there to the Wash, to the point now known as Cut End. The alternative was to dig an entirely new direct course to the North of the Haven also starting at Skirbeck Church. The Corporation chose the first option. This reduced the channel distance by 4.5 miles. However it was 1830 before the work began and 1884 before it was completed.

The first 800 yard cut was made in the central section between the far end of where the Sewage Farm is now and the Hobhole outfall. This took three years and shortened the channel by 1.5 miles. Work on the stretch past the Landfill Site was started in 1841 where a straight channel was largely achieved by fascine work, only excavating where necessary. Fascine work consists of placing bundles of sticks, known as kids or faggots, on the outside bend of the river bank to encourage silt to accumulate amongst them, this gradually straightens the channel and is a cheaper method where it can be done.

The section alongside the Haven Country Park and past the sewage works was finally straightened by fascine work in 1860. During this thirty year period the silting up of the Haven outfall through 'The Scalp' became worse and in 1868 there was one day when the tide did not even reach the Boston Town Bridge. The final new cut from Hobhole to the Wash was completed between 1880 and 1884. Three Ruston Steam Navvies were used, working side by side in the bed of the new cut. Eight locomotives, numerous horses and men were also employed. Both ends were dredged.

The first ship to sail up the new channel and into the newly constructed dock on 20th December 1884 was the 1,700 ton Myrtle with a cargo of cotton seed.

This immense engineering project took 90 years to plan and complete. In so doing it exceeded the strategic aims of Rennie. It produced a self-scouring channel, solving the silting up problems of The Haven, which still requires little dredging. It also reduced the height of the water at the Grand Sluice by 1.2m to the benefit of land drainage over a large area.

More Information: *From the Romans to B&Q a History of Wyberton*

FLOODS AND GREAT DRAINAGE SCHEMES
Richard Austin

Without any warning at 7pm on 10th November 1810 the sea banks from Wainfleet to Fosdyke were overwhelmed by a North Sea storm surge. Almost the whole of the Borough of Boston was flooded. This event prompted large investment in higher sea defences and further expenditure on drains, dykes and pumps. The cost of maintaining these is now paid for by the drainage rates levied on every house and business in the Borough.

Surges in the North Sea can occur when a very high tide, pulled up by a full moon, coincides with a north westerly gale. There were significant surges in 1953, 1978 and 2013 that caused localised flooding however the defences now in place have kept the Borough largely secure. The £102m barrier in the Haven near the port is designed to give Boston a further level of protection.

Cleansing the South Forty Foot at High Bridge, Wyberton in 1910

In addition parts of the Borough are at risk from inland water at times of high rainfall and heavy snow fall. In recent times this happened in 1947, 1977 and 1981.

In the 11th and 12th-centuries monks made some of the first efforts to protect the area by building sea banks often misnamed 'Roman' banks. In 1500 a sluice was built across the Haven near to the town bridge to control the Witham, and in 1636 the first South Forty Foot Drain was dug. This was fiercely opposed by those whose livelihood of fishing, wildfowling

The South Forty Foot taken at Wyberton High Bridge in 2019

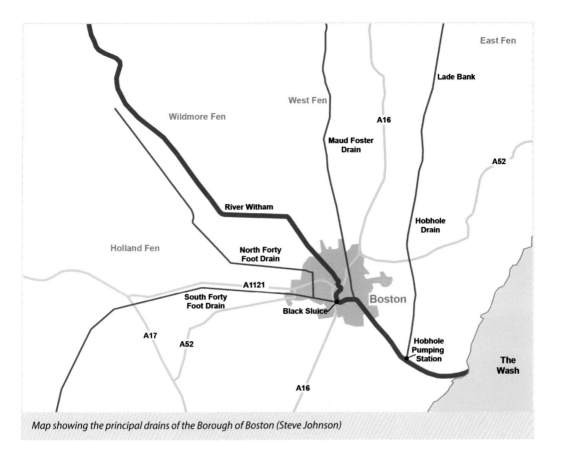

Map showing the principal drains of the Borough of Boston (Steve Johnson)

and reed cutting was threatened. They destroyed the outfall into the Haven by burning the wooden sluice gates. It is thought that is why it became known as the 'Black Sluice'.

Later, in 1658 the Skirbeck River was deepened and straightened to form the Maud Foster drain. In 1720 the North Forty Foot Drain was dug from Chapel Hill to try to improve the drainage of Holland Fen. However it was not until 1766 that there was significant protection for the low lying land between Boston and Lincoln when the Grand Sluice was built and the Witham up to Lincoln was 'canalised'.

A big scheme to reopen and extend the South Forty Foot Drain was began in 1765. Scoop-wheels powered by windmills were built to lift water from the lowest areas into this new watercourse. Steam and now electric pumps have replaced them.

The Hobhole drain was began in 1806 to drain the Fens to the north and east of Boston with Sir Joseph Banks as one of the prime movers. Peat shrinkage caused the drainage of these Fens to worsen, so in 1867 a large steam pump was installed at Lade Bank. The ornate chimney is still a feature in the landscape. In 1935 the Black Sluice and the Witham Fourth Internal Drainage Boards were established to levy the drainage rates and also to maintain and improve the system. Today they work in conjunction with the Environment Agency who are responsible for the sea defences and the major river network.

More Information: The Black Sluice and Witham Fourth Internal Drainage Boards' websites

MAPS OF MEDIEVAL AND VICTORIAN & EDWARDIAN BOSTON
Steve Johnston

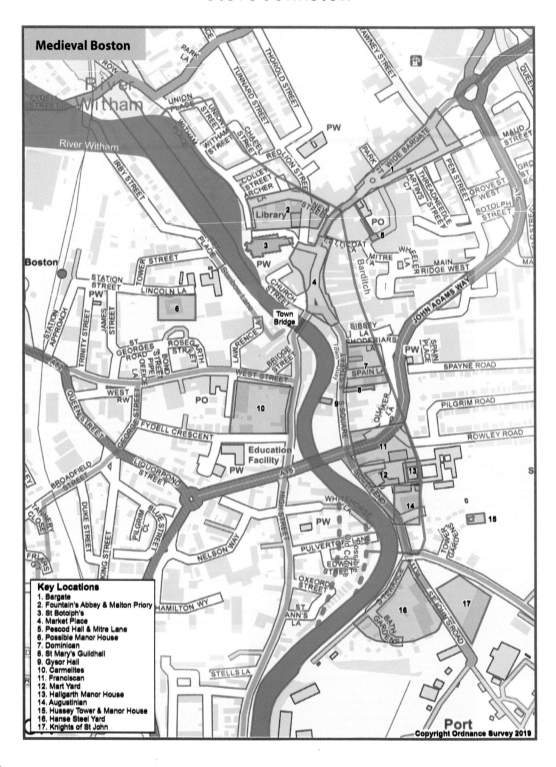

Medieval Boston

Key Locations
1. Bargate
2. Fountain's Abbey & Malton Priory
3. St Botolph's
4. Market Place
5. Pescod Hall & Mitre Lane
6. Possible Manor House
7. Dominican
8. St Mary's Guildhall
9. Gysor Hall
10. Carmelites
11. Franciscan
12. Mart Yard
13. Hallgarth Manor House
14. Augustinian
15. Hussey Tower & Manor House
16. Hanse Steel Yard
17. Knights of St John

Copyright Ordnance Survey 2019

Following the Norman takeover, Boston expanded rapidly as a trading centre to become one of England's most important medieval ports after London. During Victorian and Edwardian times, it was one of the UK's more prosperous towns due in main to its industrial innovations and enterprise that included improvements in land drainage, a new dock and the arrival of the railways.

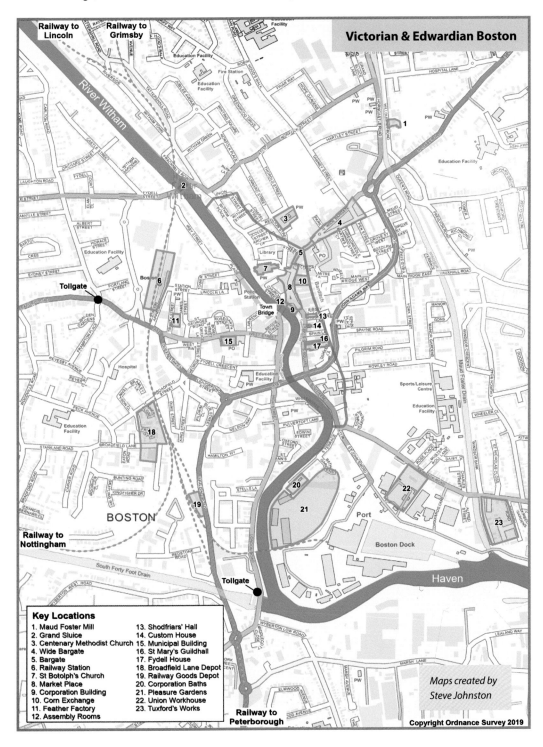

Victorian & Edwardian Boston

Maps created by Steve Johnston

Copyright Ordnance Survey 2019

Key Locations

1. Maud Foster Mill
2. Grand Sluice
3. Centenary Methodist Church
4. Wide Bargate
5. Bargate
6. Railway Station
7. St Botolph's Church
8. Market Place
9. Corporation Building
10. Corn Exchange
11. Feather Factory
12. Assembly Rooms
13. Shodfriars' Hall
14. Custom House
15. Municipal Building
16. St Mary's Guildhall
17. Fydell House
18. Broadfield Lane Depot
19. Railway Goods Depot
20. Corporation Baths
21. Pleasure Gardens
22. Union Workhouse
23. Tuxford's Works

NON-CONFORMISM IN BOSTON
Patrick Corke

When James VI of Scotland became James I of England, the Puritans wanted him to 'purify' the Church of England by appointing 'godly' ministers. However, James introduced measures to suppress the Puritans. Puritans were made up of three groups: the Presbyterians who wanted a church without bishops, as in Scotland; the Independents (Congregationalists) who wanted a church free of state control; and the Baptists who emphasised the early Christian practice of baptism.

This former chapel in Red Lion Street was used by the Congregationalists until they moved to a new and grander church building in 1850

John Wesley, founder of Methodism

The suppression of the Puritans led directly to a group inspired by Rev John Cotton leaving Boston and founding Boston, Massachusetts. Those who remained became increasingly militant, gaining the town a reputation as 'a hotbed of Independents'. One of their leaders, Mr Bankes Anderson, even became the Mayor's Chaplain in 1651.

After the Civil War the monarchy was restored and the Act of Uniformity passed in 1662. This dashed any hope of religious freedom. Mr Anderson was banned from preaching and holding public office, whilst Thomas Graham, leader of the Baptists who had been meeting since 1653 in a private house in town, was imprisoned.

Although matters settled down in 1689 when the Toleration Act was passed, trouble was never far away. In 1757 Alexander Mather and Mr Alwood, two Methodist preachers, were chased out of town. Although John Wesley was better received in 1780, Methodist services were frequently disrupted until 1789 when the Mayor agreed to prosecute those responsible for the violence.

In the following decades the town reflected the national diversity as non-conformist groups fragmented. New chapels were built which over time often passed to other groups, such as a chapel that once existed in Main Ridge. In 1802 this was the Unitarian Chapel, then in 1804 passed to the Quakers (Society of Friends) before becoming the 'Particular' Baptist's chapel and finally home to the Methodist Reformers around 1854.

A number of notable non-conformists have been associated

Centenary Methodist Church, Red Lion Street before it was almost destroyed in a fire and then rebuilt.

Founded in 1802, the Unitarians moved into the chapel pictured here in 1819. Located in Spayne Road, it is still their chapel today.

Boston's General Baptist Chapel, 2019

with the town. William Bampton who, baptised as a teenager at the 'General' Baptist chapel in the High Street, became the first missionary to Eastern India, where he and his wife took to wearing native dress. They belonged to the General Foreign Baptists Missionary Society which had been formed during the Baptist New Connection Association meeting held in the Boston chapel which William Bampton had attended.

Another, Dr William Cooke, minister at Zion chapel in 1830, became the Methodist New Connexion's thrice president and wrote a number of practical guides for Christians during the rise of Darwinism. Among those who attended his innovative training seminary was William Booth, founder of The Salvation Army, who later modelled some of the training of Salvation Army officers on his methods.

The final persecution of non-conformists came with the arrival of The Salvation Army in the town in 1878. In 1881 Captain Rees became the last non-conformist to be imprisoned. Soon afterwards Boston Corporation voted to reject petitioning the Home Secretary for more powers to ban religious groups from its streets, deciding instead to leave such matters well alone.

More Information: *The Story of Boston by Richard Gurnham; Boston and its people by George S. Bagley*

THE RAILWAY TOWN
Neil Wright

The coming of the railways had a big impact on Victorian Boston. In late 1843 interest rose throughout Lincolnshire in bringing railways into the county as part of a national spate of railway plans. The building of a railway needed the forming of a limited liability company with powers of compulsory purchase which would require an Act of Parliament. Such was the railway mania of the times that there were around a dozen schemes involving Boston put before Parliament.

The proposals that were successful were the lines to Peterborough and Lincoln as part of the Great Northern Railway (GNR) Lincolnshire loop line and the East Lincolnshire Railway's line to Grimsby, also operated by GNR. These Lincolnshire lines were opened before the GNR's mainline from London to Yorkshire and GNR located its engineering department in Broadfield Lane, where locomotives, carriages and wagons were designed.

In 1853 GNR's engineering department was moved to Doncaster on the mainline but Boston remained the headquarters of the GNR lines in Lincolnshire. As well as the Passenger Station and the Goods Yard, Boston had a civil engineer's department maintaining and repairing the track. There was also the railway locomotive depot, where many engines were based, as well as a Sacking Store which cleaned and managed sacks used in the movement of farm produce.

An ariel view of Boston station showing the GNR gasworks where the Asda Superstore is now located (courtesy of Richard Starbuck)

Passengers boarding the Skegness bound train, 2019

Train crossing the Witham near the Grand Sluice (Neil Watson Collection)

GNR even had its own gasworks producing gas for illuminating its carriages and a creosoting works that treated timber from the Baltic, imported through Boston port to produce sleepers for the railway track.

When the railway arrived it was built mainly through fields west of the town to avoid the expense of buying and demolishing houses. New streets were built between the town and the railway and many houses were occupied by railway workers. Some street names reflect the railway connection such as Station Street and Locomotive Street; James Street and Duke Street were named after Sir James Duke the director of early railways connected with Boston. West Street grew in importance as the main route to the Passenger Station.

The GNR became the largest business in Boston with about 900 employees. However that only partially compensated for taking over the traffic of the port and destroying what had been the basis of Boston prosperity for the previous eighty years. The population of Boston stagnated until the 1880s when Boston Dock was opened and the new straight channel was cut from Boston to the Wash. Boston then started to revive, though it never regained the prosperity it had enjoyed in Georgian times.

Steam engine in Boston Station (Neil Watson Collection)

More Information: *Boston, A Railway Town, by Adam Cartwright and Stephen Walker; The Railways of Boston - Their Origins and Development 1848-1998, by Neil Wright*

HERBERT INGRAM (1811-1860)
Jill Pepper

Imagine news without pictures; yet in the infancy of newspapers this was the norm. It took the imagination and determination of Herbert Ingram, a Boston man, to change the way news was presented. Born in the town on 27th May 1811, this son of a butcher was brought up in poverty after his mother was widowed. Educated at Laughton's Charity School which then operated in the south-west chapel of the Stump, he later went to the National School in Pump Square before becoming an apprentice printer to Joseph Clarke, who had premises in the Market Place.

Herbert Ingram from a photograph by John Watkins

At the age of 21 he moved to London where he met Nathaniel Cook, who later married his sister. Nathaniel's literary skills and Herbert's technical ability resulted in the two forming a partnership as printers, newsagents and stationers in Nottingham. Noticing that the sales of the newspapers in their shop rose when they carried woodcut illustrations, Herbert started a topical newspaper with copious pictures. In 1842 The Illustrated London News was born, selling at an affordable 6d a copy. The paper has remained in circulation ever since.

Ingram returned to Boston and devoted considerable time in working for the betterment of the town. He was prominent in the founding of the Boston Water Works which, in1849, provided the town for the first time with a reliable supply of fresh water. He also ensured that Boston and its port were connected to the national rail network. Moreover he was instrumental in the restoration of the Stump and paid to have the east window restored. In 1856 he stood for Parliament as the Liberal candidate in a by-election which he won with the help of Mark Lemon, editor of Punch.

During 1860, Herbert and his eldest son went on a holiday to Chicago where they took a trip on Lake Michigan. On the night of 8th September a violent storm arose and the Lady Elgin on which they were sailing collided with another schooner. There were few survivors. Ingram's body was brought back to Boston and greeted by a huge crowd. He was buried in the recently opened Cemetery where his grave is marked by a red marble obelisk. Two years later a 10 foot high marble statue of Herbert Ingram holding a copy of The Illustrated London News was unveiled in the Market Place, paid for by public subscription. In its pedestal is a carved figure of a girl holding a water-urn, commemorating his achievement in bringing water to the town.

Herbert Ingram published the first edition of The Illustrated London News on Saturday 14 May 1842

Herbert Ingram's Illustrated London News records the unveiling of their founder's memorial statue (The Illustrated London News)

Herbert Ingram's statue with figure of the water carrier within its plinth

More Information: *Herbert Ingram Esq. M.P. Founder of The Illustrated London News by Isobel Bailey*

SIR GEORGE GILBERT SCOTT (1811-1878)
Andrew Hoyle

The internationally famous Victorian architect George Gilbert Scott called Boston his 'third home'. He married his Boston cousin Caroline Oldrid in St Botolph's in 1838 and from that moment stayed in the town for part of every year. The house that was their Boston home is the large white house at the end of South Street where it joins John Adams Way. Scott was a passionate advocate of the Gothic Revival and thought that the Gothic style was the only suitable style for both secular and ecclesiastical buildings. Author Simon Jenkins has called Scott the 'unsung hero of British architecture'. A very successful English Gothic revival architect, Sir George has over 800 buildings in the United Kingdom which were designed or altered by him, including the Albert Memorial and the Midland Grand Hotel, now the London Renaissance Hotel fronting St Pancras Station.

George Gilbert's architectural connections with Boston were many. In 1837 he designed the Skirbeck Workhouse with a neo-classical façade. Known today as 'Scott House', it can still be seen set back from the Skirbeck Road. From 1845 onwards he undertook the restoration of St Botolph's, transforming the interior. His book *A plea for the faithful restoration of our ancient churches* written shortly afterwards may have been inspired by his work at the Stump.

Between 1846 and 1848 Scott designed Holy Trinity Church in Spilsby Road Boston; a wonderful Victorian building that deserves to be better known and includes a complete set of Victorian pews. Between 1869 and 1875 he restored St Nicholas' Skirbeck; the oldest of Boston's churches which has a special numinous interior. Other churches in the area designed by Sir George include the beautiful St Paul's, Fulney, near Spalding and the masterly All Saints, Nocton. Scott's first church, St Nicholas, was built at Lincoln in 1838.

George Gilbert Scott

Holy Trinity Church was one of George Gilbert's Scott's Boston projects (courtesy of Richard Starbuck)

His son, John Oldrid Scott, restored and extended Shodfriars Hall in 1873 and another son, George Gilbert Scott jnr, restored St Leodegar's, Wyberton in 1880. Sir George's grandson, Giles Gilbert Scott continued the architectural dynasty into the next century, with designs ranging from the magnificent Liverpool Anglican Cathedral to the iconic red public telephone box.

Out of favour for many decades, George Gilbert Scott's reputation has in recent years enjoyed a surge in admiration. His work on old buildings was, on the whole, based on scholarly attention to detail, and it is no exaggeration to say that he changed the way in which the country's architecture looked. Boston's collection of buildings by George Gilbert Scott is representative of the range of his work that repays careful study. He died in 1878 and is buried in Westminster Abbey.

The Albert Memorial, London (Drago Gazik on Pixabay)

George Gilbert Scott's former Boston home at the end of South Parade, Boston (Chris Sidebottom)

More Information: *Gothic for the Steam Age: An illustrated biography of George Gilbert Scott, by Gavin Stamp*

THE AUSTRALIAN CONNECTION
Jill Pepper

Inside Boston's St Botolph's church, on the north wall of its tower just a short distance from the plaque that commemorates the people from the town who helped found the United States of America, is a second plaque. This one was erected in memory of those from Boston involved in the exploration of Australasia during the 18th and 19th centuries.

Six men of the names listed sailed with James Cook. Sir Joseph Banks sailed with him on his first voyage (1768-1871) in HMS Endeavour as the expedition's lead botanist. With him went two of his servants: James Roberts (from Mareham-le-Fen) and George Briscoe (from Revesby). They helped in the collection and preservation of specimens. Cook wrote in his log: 'The great quantity of plants Mr. Banks and Dr. Solander found in this place occasioned my giving it the name of Botany Bay'.

Joseph Gilbert from Wrangle was master of the Resolution on Cook's second voyage (1771-1775). Although the Stump memorial lists him as an astronomer he used his skill as a cartographer to assist Cook with his mapping. Another local man was Richard Rollett, listed as 'Sailmaker'. He was born in King's Lynn but had lived for many years in Boston. George Gilbert, Joseph's son, whose name is not on the memorial, accompanied Cook on his third and final voyage (1776–1779). He was present at Cook's death and it was his journal, eventually published 1992, which revealed the true events leading to Cook's death.

More voyages followed and in 1795 HMS Reliance reached the Botany Bay Convict Settlement with Midshipman Matthew Flinders and ship's surgeon George Bass, on board. Flinders, from Donington, had gone to sea at 15 after reading the accounts of Cook's voyages and Defoe's 'Robinson Crusoe'. Bass,

The replica of Cook's Endeavour passing Skirbeck Church during its visit to Boston (Boston Preservation Trust)

The Australia Memorial, St Botolph's

Matthew Flinders sculpture, Euston Station, London

although born in Aswarby, had moved with his mother to Boston following the early death of his father and he was educated at Boston Grammar School. On arriving in Australia, they set out in an eight-foot boat called 'Tom Thumb', charting Botany Bay and sailing up the George River. Later they circumnavigated 'Tasmania' in HMS Norfolk, and explored the strait between Tasmania and the mainland, which, at Flinders' request, was named 'Bass Strait'.

Flinders returned to the South Seas in HMS Investigator and completed the first circumnavigation and charting of 'Terra Australis' in 1802. Flinders suggested the name of the new continent should be shortened to Australia, which was officially adopted in 1817. His second-in-command was Robert Merrick Fowler, from Horncastle. Flinders' brother, 12-year-old Samuel Flinders was appointed the ship's 2nd-lieutenant. Another of Flinders' officers was John Franklin, from Spilsby, whose parents had been married in the Stump. He was cousin to the Flinders and later became Governor of Van Diemen's Land (Tasmania) until his recall. Later, in 1848, Franklin disappeared with his ship and crew while attempting to find the North-West Passage.

The Anchor Inn and George Bass plaque located near his home in High Street

More Information: *The Australian Connection by Jill Pepper ; George Bass edited by John F Bailey*

JEAN INGELOW (1820-1897)
Jill Pepper

Jean Ingelow was born in Boston on 17 March 1820, the eldest of 10 children. Her father, William was one of Boston's bankers and the family lived in South Square overlooking the river near to what is now Haven Bridge. She loved watching the river, the sunlight glinting on the water, the vessels loaded with grain and listening to the songs of the men as they worked.

Jean Ingelow reproduced for readers of the Boston Society Magazine, 1 Nov 1899 (courtesy of Richard Starbuck)

She wrote:

"I spent many a happy hour with my brother, sometimes listening to the soft hissing sound made by the wheat in its descent, sometimes admiring the figure-heads of the vessels, or laboriously spelling out the letters of their names."

A description of childhood, from Off the Skelligs. Published 1872.

In 1825 William Ingelow's bank failed and by 1834 the family had moved to Ipswich where Jean began to write in earnest. Then around 1844 she moved to Holland Street, Kensington, London.

Her first poems were published under the pseudonym 'Orris'. It was not until 1850 that her first collection of poetry, *A Rhyming Chronicle of Incidents and feelings*, was published under her own name. Alfred Lord Tennyson, another Lincolnshire poet, remarked, "Miss Ingelow, I do declare you do the trick better than I do". They later became good friends. She also became friends of other influential writers of the time, such as the Brownings. Agatha Christie was a fan and quoted from her favourite Ingelow poem, *The Dove on the Mast* in two of her own novels: *The Moving Finger* and *Ordeal by Innocence*. It is said that Ingelow was once considered for the post of Poet Laureate. Her most popular long poem, *The High Tide on the coast of Lincolnshire*, opens with the lines -

"The old mayor climbed the belfry tower,
The ringers ran by two, by three;
'Pull, if ye never pulled before;
Good ringers, pull your best,' quoth he
'Play uppe, play uppe, O Boston bells!
Ply all your changes, all your swells,
Play uppe 'The Brides of Enderby.' "

Jean Ingelow's house was demolished as part of the Haven Bridge and John Adams Way road scheme (Neil Watson Collection)

During her lifetime she published five volumes of poetry, many running to several editions, also five novels and a verse drama. Many of her poems were set to music. In the United States she was an acclaimed author. Of her 18 works for children the most well-read was *Mopsa the Fairy*, about a boy who discovers fairies and a fairyland. The imagery and setting is still reflected today in TV favourites for the very young such as *Ben and Holly's Little Kingdom*.

While living in London, Jean Ingelow started giving 'copyright dinners'. These plain and wholesome meals were given twice a week for 12 convalescents chosen by the Kensington clergy and paid for out of the profits from her books. She died on 20 July 1897 and was buried in Brompton Cemetery, Kensington, where her gravestone commemorates both her and her parents.

The Boston in Bloom Jean Ingelow wildflower meadow and its bird boxes on waste ground adjacent to the site of her former home (Alison Fairman)

Jean Ingelow's children's story, Mopsa the Fairy, was a best seller

More Information: *Jean Ingelow Victorian Poetess by Maureen Peters*

CATHERINE BOOTH (1829-1890)
David Radford

On Christmas Day 1833, four-year-old Catherine Mumford stood inside St Botolph's with her parents John and Sarah, watching the vicar baptise her brother, John Valentine. Little did she know then that one day she would become co-founder of The Salvation Army, one of the world's most influential Christian foundations, with churches, schools, hospitals, and social programmes in more than 130 countries.

Catherine Booth (The Salvation Army International Heritage Centre)

Born on 17 January 1829 in Struston, near Ashbourne in Derbyshire, Catherine had moved to Boston when her father started a carriage business in the town at 98 West Street. He was a strong advocate of Teetotalism. Catherine, too, embraced the cause, becoming secretary of Boston's juvenile branch.

A story is told that when she was bowling her hoop along a street in Boston she saw a 'drunk' being dragged to the town's lock-up by a policeman surrounded by a jeering crowd. Coming alongside, she held his hand. Today, Salvation Army personnel are among the world's leading practitioners in the treatment of alcohol addiction.

The Catherine Booth School, Lagos, Nigeria, one of many Salvation Army Schools and hospitals around the world named after Catherine Booth (The Salvation Army, Nigeria Territory)

Catherine's mother brought her up as a Methodist. They attended the Red Lion Street Chapel but as she preferred Catherine not to pick-up the bad habits of others, she taught her at home. A biographer wrote: 'her austere mother was all the world to her daughter - her companion, her confidante, her spiritual directress, her teacher'. Catherine thrived on such subjects as the nature of sin and forgiveness, holy living and the authority of the Bible. Years later she wrote many helpful books for the Army's fledgling converts, some of which are still in print.

The Salvation Army's Dooralong, Recovery Centre, New South Wales, Australia, plays a vital role in the treatment of men and women suffering from alcohol misuse (The Salvation Army, Australia Territory)

In 1854 Catherine married William Booth, a Methodist preacher, accepting the conventions of motherhood and being a model minister's wife. That was until 1860 when two things happened. She started to preach and, when William became ill, she took over his role as church minister, not the accepted thing in Victorian England. This watershed moment for the Booths impacted on the role of women in church for generations, something still reverberating in churches today.

Within a year, Catherine and William were a team of itinerant evangelists. Eventually they moved to London and started a revival mission in the East End. By 1878 this had become The Salvation Army. W T Stead, editor of the Pall Mall Gazette and a close friend wrote in tribute, 'No one will ever know how much all that is most distinctive of the Army is due directly to the shaping and inspiring impulses of Mrs Booth'. To which Roger Green adds, 'Her vision of aggressive Christianity certainly provided a foundation for this new direction'.

Catherine died aged 60 on 4 October 1890, or as The Army says, was 'promoted to Glory'. As her funeral bier passed through London, the city came to standstill. No rank was inscribed on her coffin for she had none; instead it simply read 'The Army Mother'.

Catherine walks beside the man under arrest for being drunk in this illustration 'Befriending the Drunkard' by Victor Prout.

More Information: *Catherine Booth, A biography of the co-founder of The Salvation Army by Roger J. Green*
Blood and Fire, William and Catherine Booth and their Salvation Army by Roy Hattersley
Those Incredible Booths by John Larsson

THE PORT OF BOSTON
Neil Wright

For most of Boston's thousand years the port was on the banks of the river Witham where it passed through the town centre. Several features of this riverside port still remain. The sea-port was downstream of the town's bridge as sea-going vessels with their tall masts could not pass underneath it. Boats using the river for navigation to Lincoln would use the churchyard of St Botolph's as a quay, but after the Grand Sluice was completed in 1766 river craft used the wharf above the Sluice.

Dock and lock gates, 1914 (Boston Official Guide, 1970)

For most of history the river banks sloped down to the water with vessels being loaded and unloaded at wooden wharfs and jetties. We know little about the medieval buildings of the port. One of the few that survived until the 19th century was Gysors Hall at the north end of South Square. That was demolished in 1810 by Thomas Fydell but some stones were re-used in a new warehouse on the site, now converted into apartments.

Custom House Quay, formerly known as Packhouse Quay, was until 1884 the centre of Boston's busy port

The second great period of activity for the port of Boston was in the Georgian era with several warehouses surviving from that time. These include the second warehouse in South Square and the Sam Newsom Music Centre of Boston College. Along the north side of Spain Lane is a former seed crushing mill, and between Sibsey Lane and Craythorne Lane are two more warehouses that now form a nightclub.

Boston Docks, 1970

Harbour improvements in 1815 included a brick and stone wall that runs from the Assembly Rooms to Packhouse Quay, and a similar wall on the west bank at Doughty Quay. Both quays had public warehouses; and the tall narrow one on Doughty Quay still survives as a private house.

By the late 19th century ships could not safely rest on mud at low tide, so in the 1880s Boston Corporation built the wet Dock that is still in use today. This was built at the same time as the river from there to the Wash was straightened with a new curving channel out into the Wash. The Dock's facilities were developed to include granaries, a coal chute, ice store for fish, ship repair slipway along with offices and workshops. All of the original buildings have gone. They have been replaced by modern warehousing that is required for the storage and handling of the one million tonnes of cargo that is shipped in and out each year.

Ariel view of the modern docks opened in 1884 looking toward the Wash (Jaimaneul Freire)

THE DEEP SEA FISHING FLEET (1885-1936)
Suesan Brown

The recent creation of the Boston Docks and the much improved Haven had the potential of making Boston into an east coast fishing port on a scale similar to Grimsby. Supported by a number of influential people of the town, the Boston Deep Sea Fishing and Ice Company was formed in August 1885 by a group of Boston businessmen. The company started with seven second-hand sailing smacks and two newly built steam-screw trawlers, the Witham and the Holland both built in Hull. The company eventually phased out the sailing smacks in favour of the more profitable steam driven boats.

By 1890 Boston was a viable fishing port and the Company's 24 trawlers were operating alongside other fishing companies, such as the Boston Steam Fishing Company with whom it was to amalgamate. Fishing has always carried risks and Boston was to bear its human cost on many occasions. One such incident perhaps illustrates this most; during late December 1902 one of the Company's fishing vessels, the Grecian, was lost in Icelandic waters with all hands. The news so touched the people of the town that the Mayor immediately launched a public appeal for the families of those lost and for which the local Salvation Army band raised money by holding a torch light procession.

Landing the catch (Roy Hackford)

Steam Trawlers alongside Boston's Fish Quay (Roy Hackford)

Further tragedy struck the Boston fishing fleet when it became an early target at the outbreak of war in August 1914. In a surprise attack 16 boats were sunk. The Boston Deep Sea Fishing and Ice Company immediately suspended all fishing activities. The fishermen who were captured did not return home until the war ended. The Merchant Navy Memorial in London records the names of Boston boats and their crews lost in WWI.

In 1919 Fred Parkes joined the Company, bringing with him his four fishing boats. He lived in Wyberton and had sold his farm to buy his first fishing vessel. Wanting to secure the commercial viability of the company he proposed selling off older trawlers and buying new ones. He was opposed by other board members who claimed it would not be in the town's best interests. In 1924, having bought sufficient shares to take a controlling interest, he implemented his policy and successfully returned the company to profit and into the largest privately owned fishing fleet in the world.

In 1922 the SS Lockwood capsized whilst carrying coal to Hamburg, blocking the Haven for three months. The Boston Deep Sea Fishing Company eventually salvaged the vessel but had difficulties in recovering its costs from the Corporation. This problem, together with a general decline in the industry, led to a decision to move the Company's base from Boston to Fleetwood in Lancashire. Without enough fish being landed each day to satisfy the wholesalers, Boston began its slow decline as a viable fishing port.

The SS Lockwood with Skirbeck Church in the background (Neil Watson Collection)

More Information: *Boston Deep Sea Fisheries by Mark Stopper and Ray Maltby*

SHELL-FISHING
Suesan Brown & Shane Bageley

Shell-fishing ranks alongside salt-making and wildfowling as one of Boston's earliest occupations. It was a lucrative and dangerous occupation that once involved the retrieving of shell-fish from the exposed and treacherous sandbanks and then laying them out in shallower waters where the tide would wash them clean before they were sold on. Improvements in transportation provided easy access to the growing demands for shell-fish from the new towns and Continental Europe. This led to rapid growth which by 1868 was out of control through over-fishing. This near collapse of the industry led to it being put on a more sustainable footing. In 1898 the Boston Bailiff, Samuel Hackford noted that 288 sail and row boats were fishing in the Wash. Many of these were out of Boston.

Shell-fish are found on the shifting sandbanks and mudflats of The Wash and shrimps in the deep water channels between them. Boats have always been small, with modern boats being very versatile and able to change their rigs to suit the type of catch. When fishing for shrimp, for example, beam trawls are arrayed on booms either side of the vessel. Cockles are the main catch during the summer, although this stretches into autumn or even winter in a good year. Although for a time dredging was permitted, cockles are now harvested at low tide when they are raked out by hand. This traditional method ensures that this highly regulated industry is sustainable and that ample are left for the birds. The winter months are usually the time for mussel dredging by the boats.

An old prawn fishing boat (Roy Hackford)

Shell-fishing boats

Individual shell-fishing boats are not given an annual catch-quota, instead one is set for the entire fleet by the IFCA (Inshore Fisheries and Conservation Authority). Bedsides landing catch the fisherman manage what are called mussel 'lays'. These are designated areas that a fisherman rents where small mussels, called 'seed', are re-laid having been taken from from specific 'wild areas' of The Wash or from other places such as Morecombe Bay. These are harvested by dredging in the winter months once they have grown.

In the 1990s the increased interest in the wider environment and concerns about possible coastal flooding culminated in the realignment of the sea banks and the creation of conservation areas in the Wash and along the North Norfolk coast. One of the consequences of these changes was the disappearance of Boston's oyster farm under new sediment deposits left by shifts in the tidal pattern resulting from breaches made in the outer sea bank at Freiston.

Today, Boston's shell-fishing fleet numbers around 26 boats who must adhere to various environmental legislation in addition to IFCA regulations. However due to more effective fishing methods the annual tonnage landed is not dissimilar to that being landed at the beginning of the 20th century, still ranking Boston as one of the major suppliers of shell fish for the UK and European market.

Shell-fishing is carried out on sandbanks exposed during periods of low-tide (courtesy of Ron Jessop)

Harvesting cockles (courtesy of Ron Jessop)

More Information: *Historical and current status of cockle and mussel stocks in The Wash 2004 by CEFAS*
Boston's Fishing Fleet Facebook group

JOHNSON SEEDS
Roy Hackford

The name of Johnson's Seeds has been known for its quality seeds for almost 200 years. For many years the company was the country's leading supplier of seeds for the home gardener and commercial growers. Its lawn grass seeds provided the playing surfaces for football grounds such as Wembley Stadium and those used by Arsenal, Leeds United and Nottingham Forest to name but a few. Johnsons Seeds are now marketed by other seed companies but its trade name continues to be associated with the best in flower and vegetable and lawn seed.

Loading railway wagons (Roy Hackford)

The company was started by William Wade Johnson, a 17-year old horticulturalist. William had moved to Boston from Bucknall, it is said, as the result of a disagreement with his father. In 1820 he began selling the produce from his market garden in the town's Wednesday and Saturday markets. As a keen botanist, Johnson began growing on some of his best plants to produce seed crops. These he also started to sell from his market stall. Such was the quality and productiveness of these seeds that demand for them grew.

Over the coming years the seed side of his business developed and by the turn of the 20th century, Johnsons was the largest privately owned seed company in the UK with an expanding wholesale and general seed business throughout the world. Particular specialities were peas, beans, beet, Brussels, cabbage, carrots,

Johnson Seed Factory (Neil Wright, 1964)

turnips and seed potatoes, although a complete range of flower, vegetable and grass seeds was also marketed.

In 1911 a new headquarters, warehouse and cleaning plant were built on London Road, Boston, from where seeds of all types were processed before being despatched around the world. Such was the company's international renown that it received numerous awards from various countries. Despite the depression of the 1920s and 1930s the company continued to prosper as a prominent exporter of seeds, particularly to the United States and Commonwealth countries. This export business came to an end on the outbreak of war in 1939 and never recovered as, post-war, other countries were growing their own seeds.

Seed trial beds alongside Wainfleet Road (Roy Hackford)

In the 1960s Alfred de Bouys Johnson and his son William Wade Johnson, following a radical appraisal of the company, took the decision to re-enter the home retail market with a completely new range of pre-packed flower, vegetable and lawn seeds, along with bulbs. More than 10,000 garden centres, hardware stores, DIY shops, department stores and supermarkets began selling Johnsons products. Although its Boston warehouse has now gone, the popular Johnsons Garden Centre on the outskirts of the town is a lasting reminder of one of the world's greatest seed producers.

Johnson seeds ready for export on board the Queen Mary (Roy Hackford)

THE FEATHER INDUSTRY
Robert Fleet

The Wash with its intertidal creeks and inland fresh water marshes provided a rich habitat for wildfowl. For centuries, the wildfowlers, known as Fen Slodgers, survived by hunting them. They ate or sold the meat and sold the feathers and the soft under-layer of down for making pillows, bed-coverings, cushions and upholstery. By the 18th century, in addition to trapping the wildfowl, many of these families were breeding large flocks of geese which they brutally live-plucked up to five times a year, such was the demand for feathers.

Boston's first feather processing factory was started in 1826 by Timothy Anderson and by the end of the 19th century five of the ten feather-bed factories in Lincolnshire were located in the town. However, the draining of the fens reduced the local supply forcing the factories to import large quantities of feathers from China along with those that could be recycled from old bedding.

In 1901 Edward Fogarty acquired Anderson's Trinity Street factory with its trademark swan mounted on its roof. E. Fogarty and Company, affectionately known as Fogarty's, prospered when other feather making companies did not. By 1933, when Charles Bert Fleet became its general manager, Fogarty's was the last and only profitable feather processor remaining in the town, Bert Fleet joined the company in 1925 as a trainee under Mr Fogarty and gained a thorough grasp of the industry. Under his management the iconic 'Swan', became a trademark for quality and its factory, the UK's leading producer of feathers for the bedding and upholstery industry.

Fenland Sloggers and their catch (Pishey Thompson, 1856)

Bert Fleet (courtesy of Robert Fleet)

Forgarty's former factory in Trinity Street

Among the products it made were the filters for WW2 gas masks, manufactured from 'down' mixed with carbon. After the war Fleet created a way of re-using these feathers by inventing a revolutionary washing and steam-cleansing process. The profits from this enabled the company to relocate to a factory at Mount Bridge, Skirbeck, where water was readily available. The 'down' was sold to make the traditional 'Eider Down'.

Mr Fleet further revolutionised the bedding and upholstery industry by the introduction of his 'Curled Feather'. Taking advantage of the availability of vast quantities of chicken feather produced by the new chicken farms, Bert Fleet invented a process that 'curled' the naturally flat chicken feathers to increase their bulk and softness, mainly for use by the upholstery industry. Then in the 1960s from their new Havenside factory at Fishtoft, Fogarty's started to supply the continental quilt (duvet) that changed the sleeping habits of the nation.

Fogarty's Advertisement, 1905 (Boston Official Guide 1908)

Chinese workers with bales of feathers ready for exporting to the UK, c1930 (courtesy of Robert Fleet)

By the 1980s Fogarty's, now under the leadership of Bert's son Robert, was employing 1000 people and processing the feathers of two million chickens each week, the largest output of any feather factory in Europe. Faced with the growth of the feather industry in China, the European Down and Feather Association was formed in 1984 with Robert Fleet as its first president. In 1986 Fogarty's became part of Coloroll Plc but competition from China proved too much, and Boston's feather industry finally came to an end when Fogarty's closed in October 2018.

TAGS, LABELS AND TICKETS
John Gray

The printing of tags, labels and tickets has been big business in Boston for more than 150 years. Local companies have played a significant part in the travel industry and a leading role in the evolution of train and tram ticketing for many cities across the world. They also helped to pioneer supermarket labelling as this type of shopping developed and the need for detailed labelling of goods became ever more critical.

John Fisher and his wife (used by permission)

It began in 1849 with John Fisher who was a tailor by trade. He had difficulty acquiring tags and labels for his clothing and began to produce his own. By 1855 demand for his product reached such a peak that he opened his first printing establishment in West Street.

Things continued to flourish and George Clark bought into the business in 1870 and Fisher Clark Ltd was established with premises in the Market Place. In 1876 John Fisher sold out to George Clark who died two years later leaving an expanding business, now located in Grove Street, to his family.

In 1902 Fisher Clark acquired a factory in Norfolk Street which eventually expanded to cover 100,000 square feet. The company continued to produce tags and tickets post war, when they also became market leaders in the production of self-adhesive labels. In 1957 production space was doubled by building a new factory off Horncastle Road.

Label making in John Fisher's factory, Sleaford Road in 1857 (used by permission)

The Norprint factory (Neil Watson Collection)

The Norcros Group acquired Fisher Clark in 1960. It subsequently grew to become the largest single producer of tags in Europe. Trading under its new name, Norprint Ltd, the company developed new markets for adhesive labels. They also helped to revolutionise public transport across the world by pioneering the replacement of tickets with prepaid magnetically coated passes, for which they received The Queen's Award for Technological Achievement in 1989. The company employed about 800 people in Boston making it the town's largest private employer.

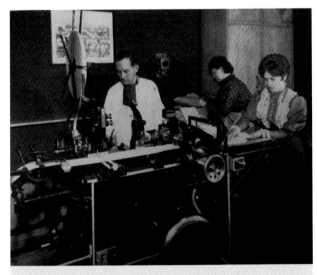
1963 Printing machine in operation (used by permission)

In 1995 it was re-organised into three divisions, Magnordata (later to become Magnadata) specialising in rail and airline travel tickets; Norprint Labels for supermarket labels and Fisher Clark for other trade labels and tags. In 2005 Norprint received a Queen's Award for its innovative identification tag to combat theft from retail outlets.

After a series of buy-outs, production was downsized to the Horncastle Road factory and in 2015 Norprint went into administration followed by Magnadata a year later. Today Coveris, on the Marsh Lane industrial Estate, still continues Boston's label printing heritage.

THE TIMBER TRADE
Richard Austin

Boston has a long history of importing timber and trading it throughout the UK. Most of this trade was, and still is, with the Baltic countries which have always had strong trading links with the town. Timber from the Baltic was used in the building of Boston's St Mary's Guild Hall in the 14th century. Over the centuries that followed, spars and masts for Nelson's Navy, floor timbers for houses and factories, telegraph poles, coal-mine pit props and railway sleepers along with wood for DIY outlets have all been imported through Boston.

Railway sleepers being unloaded at Boston Dock (engraving by C Howard, 1890)

In Victorian times large quantities of wood were required for the building of the new railways. For example, in 1848 eight vessels arrived simultaneously from the Baltic carrying railway sleepers. By 1884 when the new dock had been built and the railway link to the Midlands was operating, timber vessels that had frequently left empty could now leave with cargoes of coal. Boston's geographical position helped make it the cheapest port for importing timber into the Midlands, a situation that persisted until the 1980s.

The local companies involved included W.H. Lewin which was founded in 1859. This became Harrison & Lewin in 1880 and by 1939 had six timber yards and a storage area at the dock. J.S. Towell, another local company, was founded in 1917. A Northampton firm, E.T. Trenery and Sons, with John Atlee as Chairman, began to import timber through Boston in 1925 and in 1928 a Bristol company, May and Hassell, opened a Boston branch. This company soon dominated Boston's general timber trade. Up to the 1970s, timber yards were a very prominent sight near the docks and around the town.

Trimming telegraph poles (Calders)

The Scottish company Calders established a creosoting plant in 1896 at the dock and then in 1930 began to import and treat poles for telegraph and power lines at a new site in Wyberton, complete with its own railway sidings. In 1959 they became Calders and Grandidge. Among their present-day products are treated fence posts, rails and panels. The Great Northern Railway Company created their own sleeper treatment works at Hall Hills to the north of the town, but this was destroyed by a major fire the year that Calders moved to Wyberton.

Wood yard with railway track and crane (Calders)

After the Second World War, May and Hassell became the dominant importer of Russian timber. Cargoes arrived between July and October when the Baltic was free of ice, and timber ships queued up to be unloaded. In the 1960s it developed a riverside site on the old golf course at Fishtoft, moving their offices to there from the dock in 1982. May and Hassell acquired both Harrison and Lewin and Trenerys but were themselves taken over as trading became unprofitable. Hillsdown Holdings bought the company in 1977 which was then sold to Wickes and finally to Finn Forrest. Today it is owned by Metsä, a Finnish company which describes itself as a responsible forest industry group.

Timber ready for market (J.S. Towell)

Calder's Wood Yard from the air (Calders)

BOSTON IN THE FIRST WORLD WAR
Adam Cartwright

The sudden collapse of European countries into the massive conflict of the First World War happened over a Bank Holiday weekend in August 1914. The Boston Company of the Territorial Army were away at their annual camp in Bridlington and had to be summoned home in haste before marching to Lincoln led by their Captain Meaburn Staniland. At that time he was the youngest town clerk in the UK. The other Boston Territorial unit, an artillery battery, followed them a few days later.

On parade, men of the 4th Lincolnshire's (Neil Watson Collection)

Regular troops arrived in the town to guard the Docks and the sea bank. At sea news of the war did not reach the fishing fleet. They were surprised by the German Navy and a number of trawlers were sunk, ten of which were from Boston. Nine belonged to the Boston Deep Sea Fishing Fleet and Ice Company: *Kesteven, Lindsey, Porpoise, Walrus, Wigtoft, Skirbeck, Flavian, Indian,* and *Julian*. Those of the crews who survived, were interned until the end of the war. In all a total of 22 Boston trawlers were lost during the war, with 80 fishermen being reported as dead or missing and 91 made prisoners.

Initially Lord Kitchener's 'Your country needs you' campaign recruited just fifty volunteers from Boston, although this did rise to 250 by the end of October 1914. While there was no "Boston Pals", around 6,000 from the Borough were to serve in the armed forces. Of these more than 900 were casualties, including Captain Staniland and his brother. The heaviest losses came during the battle of Loos in October 1915 but the town was spared the devastating losses of the Somme Offensive because the units to which the Bostonians belonged were not involved.

Remembering: Unveiling Boston's war memorial, September 1921 (Neil Watson Collection)

Back in Britain there was public reaction against anything German. In the High Street there was a butchers shop owned by the German born Cantenwine brothers. This was looted and its windows smashed. The Cantenwines had been living in Boston for 23 years.

On 31 January 1916 the town experienced its first Zeppelin raid. George Cantenwine was falsely accused of signalling to it. On 2 September another Zeppelin released several bombs, but failed to destroy the Grand Sluice railway bridge. Tom Oughton, the lock-keeper's son was killed and several others were injured. In another raid George Beeton, a signalman, ran from his box to warn an oncoming train. Although the train was saved Beeton lost a leg in the bombing. George was a Salvation Army bandsman and, because he could not march, he rode a tricycle while playing his euphonium in the band's parades.

Zeppelin bomb victim George Beeton on his tricycle playing his Salvation Army euphonium (Boston SA Archives)

The Royal Flying Corps' 38th Squadron (Home Defence) had a landing ground north of Boston at Willoughby Farm from 1916 to 1918.

As the war approached its conclusion Boston became the port for prisoner exchanges. In January 1918 neutral Dutch boats brought home 600 soldiers and civilians, returning with similar numbers to Germany. There were seven more such exchanges involving over 2,500 people before the war ended in November 1918.

Remembering: November 2018, 100 years after the guns fell silent.

BOSTON IN THE SECOND WORLD WAR
Adam Cartwright

The declaration of war in September 1939 came as little surprise. The Council had already instructed the Borough Surveyor to draw up proposals for public air-raid shelters, and plans to create a new fire station were being discussed. Within hours of war being declared, 3,000 mothers with children and helpers arrived in the Market Place by bus. They were mainly from Hull and sent to billets in the surrounding villages as the town itself was considered too risky because of its port. Most evacuees had returned home by Christmas.

Survivors from Arnhem belonging to No2 Battery, 1st Air-landing Light Regiment, Royal Artillery, on parade outside the Stump on 3 October 1944 following a service of remembrance for the fallen of Operation Market Garden (Martijn Cornelissen, Arnhem Bridge: Target Mike One)

Rationing started in mid-September with the issuing of petrol coupons. Coal and food were also rationed, with some 24,000 food ration books being issued in the borough. With house building suspended the half built houses in Pilgrim Road and Eastwood Road were abandoned "for the duration". The building of a dual carriageway bypass around the town was withdrawn.

The town's older men, and those in 'reserved' occupations, became ARP wardens, firewatchers or joined the Home Guard, which was 300 strong by May 1940. Pill-boxes and defensive trenches were constructed and a team of men under the direction of the Black Sluice Drainage Board's chief engineer were tasked with blowing up key bridges in the event of an invasion. Boston's industry was placed on a wartime footing. Local families made camouflage nets for the Army, Forgarty's made the filling for gas masks and Willer & Riley's and Beulah's increased their production of canned foods.

With many Allied bomber bases nearby, Boston was an attractive night out for RAF and USAF airmen. They were frequently bussed in from their bases to enjoy the town's four cinemas, around 70 pubs, and also attend dances held at the Assembly Rooms and the Gliderdrome. The Royal Navy took over the former Union Workhouse near the docks and renamed it *HMS Arabella*.

Digging out an unexploded bomb outside Cammack's in Wide Bargate (Keith Ian Smith)

It was in June 1940 that the first bombs fell, mainly in the Wrangle area. During the raids that followed 21 were killed, 14 of them in the town itself. The worst incident occurred on 12 June 1941 when high explosive bombs fell in the James Street and West Street area. Nine people died, including a mother and her three young children. Properties including the Royal George and Loveley's bakery were destroyed. Liquorpond Street and Main Ridge also suffered damage in subsequent raids. In total at least 350 high explosive and thousands of incendiary bombs fell on Boston.

Boston men saw action in theatres of conflict, from Norway during April and May 1940 to the D-Day landings of July 1944, and in Iceland when the Territorials were sent to occupy that country, whilst its trawlers were involved in the evacuation of Dunkirk. Many serving in the RAF flew bombing raids over Germany. By the end of the war around 250 Boston men and women had been killed in the service of their country.

Warden wearing gasmask of the type fitted with a filter manufactured by Fogarty & Sons in its Boston factory (courtesy of the Home Front We'll Meet Again Museum, Freiston)

Boston's Freiston Shore was defended by an emergency coastal battery and a number of carefully sited pillboxes

More Information: *Boston Bomb Fall by K I Smith; Boston at War by Martin Middlebrook; Home Front, We'll Meet Again Museum, 3 Shore Road, Freiston Shore, Boston Lincolnshire, PE22 0LY*

FEEDING THE NATION
John Debnam

Boston and its surrounding area is the most productive agricultural region in the UK. This is the result of imaginative land management and innovation in farming methods that started with the   enclosure of parish lands during the 1700s and also investment in costly fenland drainage schemes, creating hundreds of acres of productive farmland from the area's marshy landscape. Boston and Lincolnshire now provide 60% of the nation's food.

Cabbage, cauliflower, kale, broccoli and sprouts along with potatoes and other root crops are grown in the open fields around Boston, while young plants and salad crops are produced in extensive glasshouses. Cereals, sugar beet and rape seed complete the farming mix which marks out the seasonal changes in an otherwise flat and featureless landscape intersected by drainage ditches.

Most vegetables have a relatively short life and need to reach their market in as short a time as possible. As a result one of the of the best logistic distribution networks in the country has grown up in the local area to facilitate the speedy transition from harvest to shopping basket. Among those who helped pioneer this seemless transition from

Marshalls of Butterwick food packing factory

Potato picking, 1914 (courtesy of W.Dennis & Sons)

of BOSTON
LINCOLNSHIRE

for "really good"

CANNED FRUITS
and VEGETABLES

Advertisement for Beaulah's canned fruits and vegetables (Boston Official Guide 1940)

field to customer was William Dennis (1841-1921), known as the 'Potato King', who developed the use of light railways to transport his crops to the rail network and then on to a chain of outlets throughout the country.

To meet the food crisis created by the Second World War, local farms, canning factories and wholesale merchants came together to 'feed the nation'. The result was an efficient and effective food production and delivery system that became the foundations of the modern concept 'from field to table'. When supermarkets came on the scene, the industry responded by pre-packing vegetables. Marks & Spencer established what is believed to be the UK's first pre-packed vegetable factory in two redundant Royal Air Force sheds in Butterwick.

Today the closely monitored process of food production from seed to consumer runs to a precise timetable. It is a multimillion pound business where continuous investment in mechanisation and scientifically inspired systems ensure that quality and taste is maintained from the time the produce is harvested. One of the most recent innovations has been the introduction of 'field rigs' in which the produce is packed as it is harvested.

While the number of Boston companies involved has become fewer, the number of people employed and the volume of vegetables produced has not diminished. However, it is acknowledged that the local climate cannot provide a steady supply of fresh vegetables throughout the year. To this end Boston companies have the answer in the network of growers they have forged in such places as Hampshire, Kent, Cornwall and Pembrokeshire and even in Spain and Italy to supply the vegetables when there is a local shortfall, ensuring that the supermarket shelves are always full.

Harvesting and packing in a single operation

PUBLIC PARKS AND SPACES
Neil Wright

Today Boston Borough has a great choice and variety of public open-air leisure spaces. However with the industrialisation of towns many people had little access to fresh air. In 1833 a Government Select Committee recommended providing footpaths for public exercise, and seven years later a further recommendation was for open spaces for cricket, football and other activities.

The wealthy in Boston already had such facilities. Vauxhall Gardens in Freiston Road was opened on 6 May 1815. Admission cost 6d each day, but a season ticket for a lady, gentleman and two children cost just 8s. The gardens covered two acres laid out in walks with an "elegant saloon" 62 feet long. A maze was created in 1823 and a marine grotto in about 1840. Special events were held during the season including a gala with fireworks, a flower show, a rural fete and a fancy dress ball. The Gardens closed in 1855

Free open space was provided in 1832 when a tree-lined gravel path was created on the east bank of the Haven, extending to a point opposite the Black Sluice. The Bath Gardens included two long strips of water that could be used for swimming, and in 1834 a private company built swimming baths on the marsh next to the river. Nearly all of Bath Gardens are now buried under the Riverside Quay of Boston Dock.

In 1871 the Corporation opened the large People's Park inland of the Bath Gardens. It was planted with trees, shrubs and flower beds and included areas of grass for "cricket, skittles, quoits, bowls, croquet, football, etc" as well as military drills. Next to this pleasant park Boston General Hospital was built in 1874 and new swimming baths opened on 3 May 1880. The area is now part of the Dock complex.

Bath Gardens

Children's play area (Neil Watson Collection)

To make up for the loss of the People's Park, the Corporation created the Central Park north of Wide Bargate. The site was acquired in 1919 and developed over the next few years, with flower beds, tennis courts, changing pavilions and a large grass area used for cricket. These facilities have continually been developed to meet changing recreational needs.

Until the mid-19th century burials in Boston took place in land belonging to several town churches, but then in 1855 Boston Cemetery was created on Horncastle Road at the edge of the town. The site included an entrance lodge and two identical chapels; one for Anglicans and the second for other denominations. Boston Crematorium was opened in April 1966 on an extension site to the west of the original cemetery.

Central Park, 1930

Crowds enjoying a 'beach party' event in Central Park (Boston Borough Council)

THE WASH AND ITS WILDLIFE
Chris Andrews

The Wash is a 150,000 acre square-sided estuary which forms a large indentation on the east coast of England. Characterised by vast saltmarshes and mudflats, it is internationally recognised for its important wildfowl and wading birds. It is designated as a site of Special Scientific Interest, a National Nature Reserve, a Special Area of Conservation and a Special Protection Area. There are now two RSPB reserves near Boston, at Freiston Shore and at Frampton Marsh.

RSPB Frampton Marsh Visitor Centre (Patrick Cashman)

Until the 1980s land owners regularly reclaimed more land from the Wash by constructing sea banks out in the salt marsh as the depositing silt made this possible. At Freiston Shore, for example, this was done by the Borstal Boys from North Sea Camp. (North Sea Camp had been established as a Borstal for young offenders in 1935. It became a Category D Open Prison in 1988.) However, rising sea levels and intense winter storms threatened to overwhelm these banks, potentially flooding large areas of farmland as well as nearby villages and the town of Boston itself. In order to avoid this scenario the Boston Wash Banks project was developed by the Environment Agency (EA), RSPB and other partners and the EA upgraded the outer bank.

The reclamation at Freiston was deemed too expensive to maintain so, after strengthening an inner sea bank, the outer one was deliberately breached in a process known as 'managed realignment'. The area reverted to natural saltmarsh which helped strengthen sea defences and provided a home for wildlife. It became RSPB Frieston Shore in 2002. The saline lagoon which was created became a habitat for wading birds which were displaced daily from their feeding grounds on the mudflats of The Wash by rising high tides. Thousands of birds flocking onto the lagoon provide a wildlife spectacle with birds such as the Knot, Oystercatcher and Dunlin being seen in big numbers, particularly on large autumnal high tides.

The development of Frampton Marsh nature reserve occurred in two phases. The RSPB first acquired the saltmarsh at Frampton Marsh in 1984, as it held one of the UK's largest breeding populations of Redshanks and also provided wintering grounds for an internationally significant number of Brent geese. Soon after the Millennium, the area of farmland behind the saltmarsh was bought by the RSPB, and turned into

Norfolk Coastline

The Wash

← RSPB Freiston Shore

River Welland

North Sea Camp

saltmarshes

The Haven

sea bank

bird hide

Lagoons

bird hide

bird hide

Lagoon

Visitor Centre

RSPB Frampton Marsh from the air (Jim Blaylock)

freshwater habitats to complement the saltwater marshes and mudflats. The reed-bed, freshwater lagoons and wet grassland grazing marshes were created and a visitor centre was built, including paths and bird-hides. The reserve attracts 55,000 people each year.

Knot roost, Frampton Marsh (Neil Smith)

Today, Frampton Marsh is renowned throughout the UK as one of the best places to see wading birds and wildfowl in large numbers. It boasts an impressive variety of rare visitors, including the first ever attempt by a Glossy Ibis to nest in the UK. It also provides a home for the rare Sea-aster Mining bee and the rare Slender-hare's ear plant.

Both RSPB Frampton Marsh and Freiston Shore nature reserves are open throughout the year.

Borstal Boys from the North Sea Camp at work building the sea bank.

More Information: *RSPB Frampton Marsh, Roads Farmhouse, Frampton Roads, Frampton, Boston, Lincolnshire PE20 1AY; or read more at https://www.rspb.org.uk*

BOSTON'S COUNTRY PARKS AND RESERVES
Andrew Malkin

Everyone needs an opportunity to get out, get away and breathe. Fortunately there's plenty of opportunity to do that in and around Boston as the Borough has several magnificent wild places to which residents and visitors can escape; all but one have been created since the turn of the century, the first two by the Boston Woods Trust, the last two by the RSPB and the others by the Borough Council.

Harvesting wild-flower seed from the Jospeh Banks Country Park (Boston Wood Trust)

Which Way?

Sir Joseph Banks County Park and Woods: The Boston Woods Trust area in Wyberton is made up of Westgate Wood and Jenny's Wood and has extensive wild flower meadows. There's easy access throughout this 80 acre site along hard-surface pathways. Also featured is an owl tower, a fitness trail, an orienteering course, ponds and sculptures. There's also a recently-created memorial dedicated to the County's road accident victims.

Fenside Woods: This is a 30-acre amenity just to the north of the Fenside housing estate. All-weather paths wind through an extensive area of beech trees but most English tree species are also growing here. One part of the area is retained for green burials.

These Boston Woods Trust public amenity areas have been created largely by the dedicated leadership, inspiration and generosity of Adrian Isaac and are maintained by a team of volunteers.

Witham Way Country Park: This is just a mile north of Boston's bustling town centre and is a 22-acre site off Tattershall Road with paths weaving through the woodland and meadows alongside the River Witham. It is the home of the Boston Park Run.

Havenside Country Park: This is an 82-acre linear park beside The Haven at Fishtoft with the Pilgrim Fathers' Memorial at its southern end. It's another great place to see Lincolnshire's wildlife including oyster catchers, barn owls, bats and common seals. It's also one of the best places to view boats and large vessels making their way to and from the Port of Boston at high tide.

Boston Cemetery: The 53-acre cemetery dates back to 1855. In the old part one can step out of the modern world and back in time. There are many magnificent trees that will soon be approaching 200 years old. Mown side paths enable the visitor to wander into extensive wild areas which are home to rabbits, deer, badgers and squirrels.

Bird spotting near the old chapel in the old part of Boston Cemetery

Visitors discovering more about the woods during a Boston Woods Trust's open day

Frampton Marsh: This is a newly-created RSPB reserve with visitor facilities for families and bird enthusiasts. The 428-acre site has freshwater lagoons that are a paradise for birds and watchers alike. It is adjacent to the extensive salt marsh wilderness that borders The Wash.

Freiston Shore: This is another RSPB reserve of 271 acres on The Wash marshes with brackish lagoons that attract spectacular bird life. The site is a lost Victorian sea bathing resort that once boasted a couple of hotels, most notably the 'Plummers'. In WW2 it was strongly defended against invasion. Pillboxes and other remains are now integral to the landscape.

The Owl Tower, Boston Woods

Boston Woods

IMMIGRATION
Jill Pepper

The growth of Boston over the centuries is largely the result of immigration. People have come when there has been the need for workers, or as refugees from persecution and wars. About eight hundred years ago it was the salt extraction that attracted new settlers. Since then there have been major drainage and engineering projects requiring large numbers of workers and more recently the big increase in the demand for prepacked foods and large scale vegetable cropping has stimulated an influx of workers from Eastern Europe. While population changes have sometimes caused tension, the majority making their home in Boston have added to the richness and diversity of the town's heritage and culture.

It was Count Alan from Brittany and the Norman immigrants who began making Boston a viable trading centre. However, they were not the first to set up home in the area. There is evidence of Roman occupation followed by the Saxons who established some of the early villages and the salt-making industry. The Vikings who came next gave the area the name of Skirbeck.

Eastern European traders have played an important part in Boston's economic history through the centuries and continue to do so.

Many Europeans lived and worked in Boston in Medieval time, among them Hanse merchant Wisselus of Smallenburg who was buried in the Franciscan Friary. During excavations his tomb was rediscovered and moved to St Botolph's (AM Cook, 1948)

By the 14th century Boston boasted of one of the largest ports in England thanks in part to merchants from Germany. Naturally this encouraged further immigration to support the expanding economy. Surviving tax returns from 1442-43 record they were working as weavers, shoemakers, tailors, butchers, barbers, agricultural workers and brewers. They came with their families and spoke German, French, Dutch and languages of the Baltic. The next major influx of immigrants came during the reign of Elizabeth I with the arrival of religious refugees such as the Huguenots.

During the 19th century many men came from Ireland to cut the new drains. Over time they were joined by their families or married local girls. The area of Horncastle Road, North Street and Hartley Street became known as 'Irishtown'. These people eventually became integrated into the community and no longer caused disquiet among the established families who had voiced their concerns about their livelihoods being taken away by 'foreigners'. The ensuing increase in agricultural land that followed called for migrant seasonal workers.

North Street is still a narrow lane although the Irish town to which it led no longer exists.

During WW1 and WW2 prisoners-of-war were sent to assist on the farms. Many of these men made Boston their home after the war, as the Italian names in the local cemetery bear witness.

The enlargement of the European Union and the decision to allow free movement of people between member countries led to an influx of migrant workers firstly from Portugal, then from Poland and other Baltic States. Between 2001 and 2011 the population increased by 9,000, a rise of 15.9% which made it the highest rise in the country. Despite social tensions, protests and the overwhelming 2016 Referendum vote to leave the EU, the town's prosperity seems to have increased with many of the immigrants setting up shops and helping to bring new life into the Borough.

The same shop, past and present (Chris Sidebottom)

More Information: *The Catholic Church in Boston by Martin Middlebrook*

FYDELL HOUSE AND THE BOSTON PRESERVATION TRUST

David Radford

In 1935, the fate of Fydell House in South Street was in the balance. A consortium from Birmingham was planning to demolish it in favour of a housing development. The loss of the 'grandest house in town' so alarmed the Vicar of Boston, Canon A.M. Cook and other concerned activists, that they launched an appeal to buy it. The outcome not only resulted in the house being saved, but in the creation of the Boston Preservation Trust as a limited company, whose aim to save other historic buildings in the town and bring them back into meaningful use continues to this day.

Fydell House was given its name by Joseph Fydell, a merchant who traced his family's associations with Boston back to William Fydell, an apprentice to Alderman Thomas Marcall in 1676. Joseph began to establish himself as one of Boston's more successful merchants around 1717 when he added to his warehouses a yard in Spain Lane. In 1726, the house then owned by Samuel Jackson became available. Joseph quickly made the purchase. In work carried out subsequently he had the date and his initials embossed on the lead work.

Fydell House

From research into the house's origins by A.A. Garner, it has been established that it was probably built around 1700 for the Jackson family. They were Mercers: dealers in textiles, silks, velvets and other expensive cloths. Prominent in Boston, one of the family, Edmund Jackson had been Mayor in 1668 and 1678 but the decline of the cloth trade eventually led to the house being sold. For Joseph Fydell, however, the ownership of such a fine house immediately raised his social standing although ultimately it proved to be an expensive investment.

The American Room

Passing down through several generations, including Robert Fydell who almost lost the house when he was declared bankrupt in 1738 and his son Richard who served at Boston's MP and three times Mayor, Fydell House remained a family home until 1816 when it was leased to tenants. These included Henry Rogers, lord of the manor of Freiston and Butterwick and Francis Yeatman, a wine merchant, whose skill as a gardener meant that the garden at the rear of the house was acclaimed 'the finest garden in the borough'.

The garden

US Ambassador to the UK, Joseph Kennedy is pictured here with some children outside Fydell House during his 1938 visit to Boston when he dedicated the American Room. Joseph Kennedy is the father of US President John F Kennedy.

Following its purchase from the Fydell family by the Boston Preservation Trust in 1935, Fydell house has served a number of uses. It has strengthened Boston's link with the USA. In the 1930s there were a number of visits to Boston by prominent Americans culminating in one by US Ambassador Joseph Kennedy in 1938, who dedicated the American Room. Joseph was father of US President JF Kennedy.

During WW2 the house was the base for the Women's Voluntary Service. After the War it became the base for the Adult Education Programme and the Workers Educational Association. It was known as Pilgrim College and hosted a wide range of courses. Today, this role is mainly filled by Boston College.

The Boston Preservation Trust continues to serve the town through its balanced approach to preservation and the practical conservation of Boston's historic buildings. Fydell House is a fine example of this approach. Not only is it the Trust's offices, a venue for educational courses, events, lectures and formal occasions, it also welcomes visitors who want to come and admire a magnificent historic house and its famous American Room.

More Information: The Fydells of Boston & The Grandest House in Town by Arthur A. Garner; Boston (Britain in Old Photographs) by David Cuppleditch; Boston, Lincolnshire. Historic North Sea port and market town by John Minnis & Katie Carmichael.

— SHODFRIARS HALL AND OLD MOTHER RILEY —
Robert Barclay

The name Shodfriars is derived from the order of friars who lived nearby and who wore shoes (shod friars) as distinct from others who went barefoot or wore sandals (discalced friars). Shodfriars Hall is, in fact, two conjoined buildings of differing architectural styles. The first is the magnificent black and white jettied timber framed building which dominates South Street. The other is an equally impressive red brick building, whose main façade is almost hidden from view in Shodfriars Lane. While not much is known about the history of the timber-framed structure it possibly dates from the end the 14th century and was known as the 'Golden Hows'. One of its other names was the 'Old Flemish House'. Some of the earliest rental book evidence suggests is was used by Boston's Corpus Christi Guild.

Shodfriars Hall, 1900 (courtesy of Richard Starbuck)

Shodfriars Hall, 2018

Between 1873 and 1875 the building was given a Victorian face-lift by John Oldrid Scott, son of George Gilbert Scott, the famous architect. This work, commissioned by the Conservative Club included the building to the rear. Assisted by his brother George, and built in the Gothic Revival style, often used by their father, it included a stage and entertainment space. After the Conservative Club moved to new premises this became the Shodfriars Theatre. The last performance there took place in 1929, after which the building has had various other uses: a nightclub, a restaurant and snooker hall.

Among the famous acts that trod the boards at Shodfriars during its heyday was Old Mother Riley, played by Arthur Lucan. Born Arthur Towle in Sibsey in 1885, Arthur had moved to Boston when he was five. Later as an eight-year-old he earned pocket-money at Shodfriars Theatre sweeping floors and selling programmes. Having gained a taste for theatre, Arthur ran away from home when he was 14 and joined the 'Musical Cliftons'. During a trip to Dublin he secured the part of the Grandmother in the pantomime 'Little Red Riding Hood'.

In 1913, after a whirlwind romance Arthur, then aged 28, married the pantomime lead, 16 year old Kitty McShane. He became 'Arthur Lucan' and toured with his wife as Old Mother Riley, an Irish washerwoman, and her teenage daughter, Lily. Success led to theatre tours as far afield as New Zealand, a Royal Command performance in 1934, and the release of their first film in 1937. In recent years the special comedy genre he pioneered has continued in TV's acclaimed 'Mrs Browns Boys' series starring Brendan O'Carroll as Mrs Brown with his wife, Jenny Gigney, who plays his daughter Cathy.

A coffee shop and project information centre have recently been opened in Shodfriars. Guided tours of this prominent historic building are available. Plans to reinstate Shodfriars as a theatre and as a multi-purpose events venue are being considered.

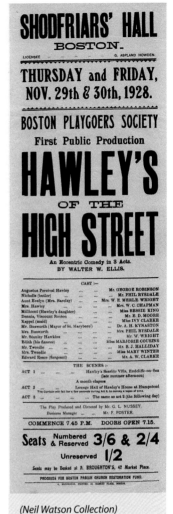

Old Mother Riley double act: Arthur Lucan and his wife Kitty McShane (Neil Watson Collection)

John Oldrid Scott redesigned Shodfriars Hall and created a Gothic style extension to the rear as part of an ambitious rebuild for the Boston Conservative Club

Shodfriars Hall Cafe

THE MAUD FOSTER MILL
James Waterfield

"Friday last, as the workmen were employed in fixing the sails to the mill just erected on the side of Maud Foster's Drain, near Bargate bridge, Skirbeck, one of them fell from the scaffolding, and would have been precipitated to the ground, had he not caught hold of a rope, of which he was enabled to keep his grip for full three minutes, till rescued from his perilous situation by being drawn into the mill through one of the windows". So reported the local press in September 1819 as Boston's newest mill neared completion. The last of the town's 15 windmills, the sails of the Maud Foster Mill still turn today.

Maud Foster Mill, Willoughby Road, Boston (Bryan S. Graves)

Maud Foster Mill, sometimes known as Reckitt's Mill, was built in 1819 for Quaker brothers Thomas and Isaac Reckitt of Wainfleet by a local firm, Pacey and Watmough. The work was overseen by Messrs. Norman and Smithson of Hull, who had a reputation for constructing the most up-to-date windmills. The machinery was probably made in a Hull foundry and sailed down the coast to Boston. The wood used in its construction would have been selected at Boston's quayside from timber imported from Archangel, Russia.

When the business failed it was sold and as a consequence of their insolvency the brothers were excluded from the Society of Friends in 1837. Mrs Reckitt, their mother, told a meeting of the Quakers that if other members had been more helpful, they should not have ended up as they did. The family moved to Hull where they cleared their debts and had their Quaker membership restored. Trading

Milling machinery, Maud Foster Mill, Boston (Bryan S. Graves)

first as Reckitt's then Reckitt and Colman, it is today Reckitt Benckiser, producing Dettol, Calgon, Strepsils and other well-known household brands.

In 1837 the mill entered a period of new ownership starting with Jonathan Dent and including Cookes of Digby, the Jessop family and finally the Ostler family. A steam engine from Tuxford's of Boston was added to drive a bone mill and another for grinding cement clinker, but these proved unprofitable and the engines were altered to grind flour. Tuxford's own eight-sail windmill stood at Mount Bridge.

In 1916 new regulations stopped the production of white flour, leaving the mill to produce animal feed only. After WW2 it became difficult to find the material to carry out repairs to the rotten sails and in 1948 milling ceased. A limited restoration to celebrate the coronation of Queen Elizabeth II was paid for by the Reckitt family in 1953 but by 1987 the mill was in a very poor state.

Having been purchased by the Waterfield family, the present owners, the Maud Foster Mill was restored to full working order and reopened in 1988. It is now one of a handful of working windmills in the UK where visitors can watch the mill at work and purchase flour and other products.

The flour produced is collected in sacks ready for distribution (Bryan S. Graves)

The Gallows Mills shown here were demolished to make way for Boston's Dock (Boston Society Magazine 1900)

More Information: *History and Guide to the Maud Foster Mill by Luke Bonwick*

HEALTH CARE IN BOSTON THROUGH THE AGES

Dr Martyn Walling and Dr Ken Hines

Only Pilgrim Hospital rivals St Botolph's church tower for a place on Boston's skyline, symbolic of the importance that is now attached to health care. Before the 1900s people relied extensively on quackery, prayer, leeches, herbs and even poisons such as mercury, arsenic and phosphorous. However during the 19th Century there were rapid changes with scientific methods and anaesthetics being increasingly adopted. In addition better nutrition and welfare led to an improvement of the general health of the population.

Today doctors and other health care professionals provide a wide range of medical services, many based in new, purpose-built medical centres. Pilgrim Hospital, which received its first patients in 1971, now includes an acute Mental Health Unit, an Intensive Care Unit and a very busy Accident & a Emergency department; ambulances along with an air ambulance support this health care provision. Health Care in its several forms now employs the greatest number of people in the area.

Boston General Hospital

Before 1948 health care was not free and many people relied instead on chemists or druggists for help. Most doctors worked in small surgeries, frequently part of their homes and also cared for their patients in hospital. Doctors in rural areas may have found themselves paid in kind, with a chicken for example. At the time of WW2 Boston's hospital had just one consultant surgeon, one physician/ paediatrician and one anaesthetist and a small team of nurses.

St John's Almshouses alongside the Maud Foster Drain, Willoughby Road

Pilgrim Hospital, Boston

The earliest known hospital in the town was the 'Hospital of St Leonard', established in 1220 and run by monks. It was renamed 'St John the Baptist Hospital' in1230 and taken over by the Knights Hospitallers. In 1542 this passed to the Duke of Suffolk who later built almshouses on the site, retaining the name. Today these almshouses are managed by a charitable trust. The Hospitallers also had a hospital in Skirbeck. Boston's Union Workhouse was built on part of its site in 1836 and included a small hospital ward.

A cholera epidemic in 1832 led to the creation of a temporary hospital in a warehouse, although it was not until 1874 that Boston had its own General Hospital. This was opened in two cottages in Irby Street in 1874 and two years later moved to a new, 22-bed building beside Bath Gardens. Nearly a century later this was replaced by the Pilgrim Hospital.

In order to manage dangerous diseases on ships using the port, an isolation hospital was set up in 1887 in White House Lane with two wards dealing with plague, cholera, yellow fever and other infectious deseases. A sanatorium for people with tuberculosis opened in 1922 at Norton House, later to form part of the London Road Hospital. Wyberton West Hospital, which opened in 1938 and was used as a receiving centre for evacuees, is mainly remembered as a Maternity Hospital. Other treatment centres, now gone, included Allan House on Carlton Road and Holden House in South Square both of which were used by the Red Cross and St John Ambulance for the rehabilitation of troops during WW1.

Lincolnshire Air Ambulance (courtesy of Lincolnshire & Nottinghamshire Air Ambulance)

SPORTING HEROES
David Radford

No story of Boston would be complete without reference to its sporting heroes who have achieved local, national and international recognition. Among them are many footballers, no fewer than six Olympians and two ocean rowers.

J.W. Julian, Arsenal's first professional club captain, 1891

Bill Julian who was born in Boston in 1886, played for Boston Town before joining Arsenal in 1899. When the team turned professional in 1891 he had the honour of being its first captain. Bill later played for Spurs and in 1895 became the British Ladies' Team coach. Another Boston born footballer who started his career at Boston Town was Richard Leafe (1891-1964). His £2,000 transfer fee from Sheffield United to West Ham in 1922 was a record for the time. Chris Woods, from Swineshead, joined Nottingham Forest in 1976 as a 17-year-old and later went on to play for clubs such as Norwich City, Glasgow Rangers and Colorado Springs, USA, which he joined in 1996.

Ray Tinkler was a well-known FA referee, serving from 1961 to 1976 with first division teams both at home and abroad. He was also an FA Councillor and chairman of the Referees' Committee.

In the field of motorcycling Bernard Codd (1934-2013), a former Boston Grammar School pupil and Dickie Dale (1927-1961) were winners of the Isle of Man TT races. Dickie in 1951 and Bernard in 1956. Neil Kent, another of Boston's TT racers won the Mountain course and in 2010 received the John Goodall 'Spirit of the Manx' Award, created to recognise sportsmanship, endeavour and commitment. Neil died following an incident while on a TT practice run in 2011. Motorcycle trials champion Emma Bristow won the first of many European and the World Women's Trials Championships in 2014.

Dickie Dale

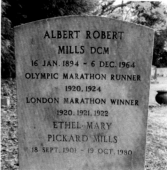

ALBERT ROBERT
MILLS DCM
16 JAN. 1894 - 6 DEC. 1964
OLYMPIC MARATHON RUNNER
1920, 1924
LONDON MARATHON WINNER
1920, 1921, 1922
ETHEL MARY
PICKARD MILLS
18 SEPT. 1901 - 19 OCT. 1980

Albert Mills, Olympian and London Marathon winner is buried in St Leogear's churchyard, Wyberton

The town has had its share of Olympians starting with Albert Robert Mills who ran in both the 1920 and 1924 marathons. England's goalkeeper Michael Pinner who began his football career at Boston Grammar School and played for such clubs as Manchester United and Chelsea appeared for Great Britain in the 1956 and 1960 Olympic Games. Swimmer Melanie Jane Marshall participated in both the 2004 and 2008 games. She also won six Commonwealth medals in 2006 and has since become an award winning swimming coach to Adam Peaty who took an Olympic gold in the Rio games of 2016.

Melanie Marshall (courtesy of British Swimming)

Boston born hockey players Hannah McCleod and Christa Cullen were members of the 2012 UK Olympic bronze medal winning team. They also took gold at the 2016 Rio games. Both have since been honoured with the MBE for services to hockey.

There are many other sporting heroes, such as footballer Jack Manning and cricketer Cyril Bland and two mighty seafaring brothers Steve and Mick Dawson. The brothers attended Carlton Road School. They later became Royal Marines and ocean rowers. Steve Dawson has rowed the Atlantic in both directions on several occasions and his brother Mick became the first to row the Pacific Ocean with Chris Martin in 2009.

Steve Dawson battling a stormy mid-Atlantic sea while his crew mate tries to keep the camera steady to snap the moment (Bob Munslow)